Sand In Boots

Lindsay Trish

Copyright © 2024 by Lindsay Trish

All rights reserved.

No portion of this book may be reproduced in any form without written permission from the publisher or author, except as permitted by U.S. copyright law.

Contents

1. Chapter 1 — 1
2. Chapter 2 — 9
3. Chapter 3 — 17
4. Chapter 4 (smut) — 23
5. Chapter 5 — 27
6. Chapter 6 — 35
7. Chapter 7 — 42
8. Chapter 8 — 47
9. Chapter 9 — 54
10. Chapter 10 — 61
11. Chapter 11 (smut) — 67
12. Chapter 12 — 71
13. Chapter 13 — 78
14. Chapter 14 — 86
15. Chapter 15 — 92

16. Chapter 16   96
17. Chapter 17   104
18. Chapter 18   111
19. Chapter 19   117
20. Chapter 20   122
21. Chapter 21   130
22. Chapter 22   136
23. Chapter 23   141
24. Chapter 24   147
25. Chapter 25   151
26. Chapter 26   157
27. Chapter 27   162
28. Chapter 28   167
29. Chapter 29   173
30. Chapter 30   179
31. Chapter 31   186
32. Chapter 32   191
33. Chapter 33   197
34. Chapter 34   204
35. Chapter 35 (smut)   210
36. Chapter 36   217
37. Chapter 37   223
38. Final Chapter   229

Chapter 1

I never thought I was made for a particularly extraordinary life. Ever since I was a little girl, all I had ever wanted was to be a mom and a wife. I had often found my value to be in the eye of the person looking at me and that might explain why I hadn't been feeling so confident lately.

When I first got pregnant with Ellie, I really thought, for a second, that I could have it all. My never ending optimism had led me to believe that having a baby would make her dad grow up and be the man I wanted him to be. That we, one day, would be one big happy family. But Josh never wanted that. He had left me to fend for myself and our unborn child at eight months pregnant. It had taken me months to heal from that. I'd had to piece my heart back together, and I did. And now, three years later, I could genuinely say that I was doing alright. I had gotten a job as a secretary in a clinic and my daughter was growing to be smarter, funnier and more beautiful every day. I had made incredible friends here, in Burlington, and I could truly say that I was proud of the road I had taken. Given, my life was not the one I had imagined growing up. The guy I had thought would be my prince charming had turned into a frog real fast and my dating life as a 22 year old single mom was pretty dull, but still. I wouldn't have traded my life for anyone else's. Especially considering what came next.

****

I got up at 6:30 that morning and quickly got Ellie ready for daycare. As I walked out the door, I stumbled across my neighbor, Ms. Brown.

"Aren't you the cutest thing", she said, pinching Ellie's left cheek and making her giggle.

"Are you still okay to watch her tonight, Ms. Brown?" I asked.

"Of course! Aren't we going to have a ball, little Ellie? Now, tell your mama she has nothing to worry about!" She said cheerfully.

"Thank you, I'll bring her by around 6! Have a good day Ms. Brown," I said, rushing down the stairs. I loved that woman so much. I don't know how I could've gotten to where I am today without her. Ever since Ellie and I had moved in next door, Glenda Brown had always been willing to help us out. Whether it be watching Ellie for a few hours, cooking us dinner once in a while to give me a break or bringing us groceries every time she goes to the store, that woman had always been willing to help. And I was thankful.

I dropped Ellie off at daycare and when I got to work, Jared was already waiting for me in the parking lot.

"Aubrey! Are you excited?" He asked, visibly a lot more excited than I was.

"Yeah, sure," I chuckled.

"Oh, you'll love it! Getting a couple beers with the boys, watching the game, you'll wish every Friday night was like this!"

"Don't overdo it Jared," I chuckled awkwardly.

"You'll get to meet my friends too, which I am SO excited about!"

"Yeah? What if they don't like me?"

"Since when do southern guys not like pretty girls?" He winked. I sighed and pushed his shoulder playfully, rolling my eyes at him.

"Alright, time to clock in Dr. Munsen."

****

The day went by fairly quickly. Jared kept coming to see me in-between patients to remind me of how excited he was for me to meet his friends. He had moved here from Tennessee for school and had ended up getting an internship here in Vermont. One thing had led to another and seven years later, he was still here, telling people every now and then how this was his "last year in Vermont" and that he was "getting ready to move back to Tennessee" without ever making concrete plans about it. I was a little nervous to meet his friends. Not because I feared they wouldn't be nice or anything like that, but just because he spoke so highly of them. It was one of these things where if you don't get along with the friends, it might change your whole relationship and I did not want that to happen. Jared was the one who had gotten me the job at the clinic once he found out I was a single mother trying to make ends meet. He was one of my closest friends. I owed him a lot and I wanted to make him happy.

I had no idea who his friends were. He had mentioned them a few times; Jesse, Ernest, and Morgan- but had not wanted to give me any more information on them. "No last names, no looking them up on social media, I don't want you to have any preconceived ideas" he'd said to me. I was about to find out why.

I went to pick up Ellie around 5 and gave her a quick bath before dropping her off at Ms. Brown's for the night. I wasn't a big baseball fan. I have to admit I don't think I'd ever watched a game before that day, but I was still excited to get out of the house. I had agreed to meet Jared at his place. I pulled into his drive-way but barely had time to get out of my car before he came out of the house, ready to go.

"C'mon Aubrey, we gotta leave if we don't want to be late!" he yelled, already sitting in the driver's seat of his gray chevy pick up truck. I opened the passenger door and got in.

"I can't wait for you to meet my friends," he said, pulling out of the driveway. "And, we have really good seats too! VIP box baby!"

I looked at him shocked.

"What do you mean VIP tickets? That must have cost you a fortune! I'll never be able to pay you back!"

"Girl you're not paying me back. That's not even an option, regardless of the seats I won't take a penny from you. I wanted you to come to the game and meet my friends, it's not about the money. Plus I had to get box seats, can you imagine the commotion it would've caused to be seated with everybody? No privacy, people coming up to us all night?"

I looked at him confused.

"Huh? Why would people come up to us?" I asked, trying to understand what he meant by that. He chuckled and scratched his neck awkwardly.

"It's not- I just wanted to spoil you. And my friends. Nothing weird, just me being my usual generous self, that's all," he said, brushing off my confusion.

"You're being weird," I said. He dismissed my comment and turned on the radio.

When we got there, the stadium was already packed. The minute I got out of the car, I felt the emotional frenzy emerging from the parking lot. People pre-gaming, drinking beer in camping chairs and placing bets on which team was going to win- or whatever people bet on when they watch baseball. I suddenly realized just how good it felt to be out and about, just spending a fun night with a friend. Thank you Ms. Brown, I thought to myself.

We got our tickets validated and walked into the stadium, looking for our seats.

"Looks like they got here before us!" Jared said, clearly impatient to see his friends. He grabbed me by the arm and started walking in their direction, dragging me through the busy crowd. I was trying my best to keep up with him when I tripped over a chair that had been taken from the bar and left right by the side of our box.

It was like an out of body experience. I could already see myself busting my two front teeth over the hard concrete floor or breaking my leg getting caught in the chair. I was almost on the ground when I felt a strong hand grab me by the arm and pull me right back up.

"Careful there", the voice said in a rough southern accent, "damn near broke your pretty face over that chair."

I looked up to see who my knight in shining armor was. All I could see was how beautiful his eyes looked. Like the sky on a sunny cloudless day. A blue like the one you see at the beach in the middle of august where the sea meets the horizon. He smiled at me -a slightly crooked smile with a somewhat coarse mustache resting on his upper lip. His wavy hair was mid-neck length and was covered by a black backward cap. My heart skipped a beat. Who was he? I closed my mouth, just now realizing how long I'd been staring at him.

"Um, yeah, thank you", I mumbled, probably inaudibly over the noise of the crowd. He smiled and nodded his head.

"Morgan!" Jared yelled, bringing me right back down to planet earth. "How've you been brother, how's the touring life been treating you?" He asked as we walked into our box and heading towards the private bar. Touring life?

"Yeah, not too bad man. Trying to keep myself out of trouble y'know", he answered scratching the back of his head. "Who's this little number?" he asked, pointing towards me with his chin.

"Oh, that's Aubrey," Jared said nonchalantly. What an introduction.

"Better than the last one," he said, winking at me.

"We're not dating," I said dryly. "I'm his secretary."

"And friend," Jared added, squeezing my shoulders, trying to make up for his rough introduction.

"Oh, so you're the secretary," he said. "Yeah, we've heard about you."

Jared nudged him, semi-subtly, probably thinking I wouldn't notice. I furrowed my eyebrows.

"You have?" I asked. He looked at Jared, who gave him a warning look, and chuckled.

"Well, I think I better keep my mouth shut," he said before turning to the bartender to order his drink. "Hi darling, whiskey, neat." God he's hot. Jared turned to me.

"Come, I'll introduce you to the rest of the gang." He pulled my forearm lightly, walking towards two other guys who were already talking to each other. One was bigger, blond haired and blue eyed. The other one was heavily tattooed, tall, dark haired. Also incredibly hot.

"Jesse this is Aubrey, Aubrey, Jesse," he said as the tattooed guy shook my hand delicately.

"Pleased to meet you," he said, his voice a lot softer than I had imagined and his accent not quite as defined as Morgan's.

"And I'm Ernest," said the other guy, beaming at me. I nodded my head slightly and smiled back at him. We made small talk for a bit, but it wasn't too long until the guys started talking amongst them. I turned my head discreetly to see what Morgan was up to. Still chatting up the barmaid. Should I go talk to him? I turned my head back. Jared was now deep into a heated debate about which player was going to be this year's MVP. I turned around and started walking towards Morgan.

"Hey. Where are you going?" Jared asked.

"Just getting a drink. Am I allowed, daddy?" I said mockingly. He rolled his eyes at me and returned to his conversation. I giggled and went to sit down at the bar next to Morgan.

"What's your poison?" He asked me.

"Tequila"

"Hey sugar, two tequilas please," he told the bartender. She stared me down from head to toe and turned around to get our drinks, probably disappointed I had crashed their little party.

"Don't cowboys drink whiskey?" I said playfully. He smiled to himself.

"Only if you drink it with me," he answered.

"Sure tang baby," I said in his accent. He chuckled.

"Hey darling, how about two whiskeys instead?"

Hi darlings, this is a short chapter just to get you started on this new fanfic I've been writing! Hopefully you like it, feedback is always welcome

Ps: If you're reading this fic after it's been completed and like it, please feel free to vote on the chapters! Its still makes me really happy to know people still enjoy this story <3

XO

LadyBug

Chapter 2

The first drink went down smoothly. So did the next three. I tried to get off the bar stool I was sitting on to go to the bathroom but gravity brought me down almost immediately.

"Careful baby," Morgan said, grabbing me semi-roughly. "I already saved you twice tonight. you can't keep falling down like that," he chuckled, his eyes squinting slightly as he smiled. He did not look nearly as drunk as I was. That"ll teach me to try to keep up with southern guys.

"I gotta go use the restroom," I slurred, losing my balance slightly, holding on to the bar.

"What's going on here?" I flinched. I turned around and saw Jared standing behind me with a concerned look on his face.

"Hiii, I was just telling Morgan I need to go to the bathroom," I said, suppressing a hiccup. He frowned and looked at Morgan.

"What the fuck did you give her?" He snapped, obviously angry at how drunk I was.

" I didn't give her anything. We drank a little whiskey, got to know each other a little better."

"She's drunk off her ass!" Jared yelled.

"Woah there, I'm a big girl. I can take care of myself," I answered, holding on to Morgan's shoulder for balance.

"Give me your phone," he said, grabbing it out of my hand semi-roughly.

"Don't be ripping shit out of her hands like that man, that's not cool," Morgan said. Jared didn't bother to answer. The look he gave him said enough.

"I am calling Glenda Brown. You can't go pick up Ellie like this."

"Who's Ellie?" Morgan asked.

"My daughter."

"You're a mom?" He asked. I nodded yes.

"It's ringing. Everybody shut up," Jared said dryly.

"I'm a dad too," Morgan whispered.

Is he? Well, that I did not expect. I had so many questions, and I wanted to ask him about his kid, but Ms. Brown seemingly picked up.

"Hi Ms. Brown, this is Jared, Aubrey's friend... Yes, the doctor... Aubrey has seemingly had a bit too much to drink. Is there any way you could keep Ellie until tomorrow morning? I would be able to come pick her up at 9... Thank you Ms. Brown, you are an absolute angel... Yes, 9 o'clock on the dot! I will see you tomorrow!" he said right before hanging up.

"Alright, that's enough now, you're coming home with me until you sober up," he said. "Can I get a water bottle for her please?" he asked the barmaid. She nodded quickly before handing it to him.

"I'm good, Jared. I wanna stay. Plus, there's only 40 minutes left to the game. And these are really good seats," I mumbled. He looked at me and then looked at Morgan. He sighed.

"Alright. But no more drinking, Aubrey. I'm serious. I'm surprised you're even still standing," he said. "Please keep an eye on her this time," he told Morgan.

"Will do, sir," Morgan answered, giving him a military salute. Jared rolled his eyes and walked back to his seat.

"Finally," I said. "I felt like I was about to get grounded."

Morgan chuckled into his beer.

"That's just 'cause he likes you and he thinks I'm trouble."

"Well, are you?"

"Am I what?" He asked.

"Trouble?"

"Depends on who you ask."

"I'm asking you," I answered.

"You're drunk," he said, looking directly into my eyes. Gosh he was beautiful. It was like I could get lost in his eyes. Like the rest of the world just stopped moving when he looked at me.

"You're drunk too," I responded. He chuckled.

"Not even a little bit," he said, moving a little bit closer to me. Close enough for me to detect the sweet smell of tobacco on his breath. "But I don't need to be drunk to tell you you're pretty," he added. My heart skipped a beat. I was really hoping he would kiss me right then and there. He turned around quickly, looking at Jared who I then realized had been staring at us. He looked back at me. I unconsciously bit my lower lip, anticipating what he was going to say or do next.

"You're the one who's trouble," he said.

"What do you mean?" I asked. He shook his head.

"Hey darlin' can I get a whiskey?' He asked the bartender. I looked at his half full beer. He looked back at me. "I mean that you're a very pretty girl, which I'm sure you already know, and that normally I'd try to kiss you and probably even try to get you into bed with me, but Jared's a good guy."

"What does that have to do w- Wait do you like Jared?!" I asked.

"Girl, how drunk are you?" He laughed, nearly choking on his beer. "I don't like Jared, Jared likes you. Why do you think he brought you here tonight?"

"I don't know, 'cause we're friends?" I shrugged. "I don't like him like that."

"Doesn't matter, he does."

"You don't know our dynamic. He's just protective of me, like in a big brother kind of way," I said, waving at Jared. He waved back, seemingly confused.

"Girl, stop waving at him, you look suspicious as hell," he chuckled, putting my hand down.

"Look, I'm not into him like that so, problem solved!" I said. "Now please, kind sir, will you escort me to the bathroom?" I asked. He looked outside of our box as if he was trying to see how busy it was.

"I'd rather not," he said. What the hell?

"Uh, okay then. Thanks I guess," I said dryly.

I turned around and left the box to go to the restroom area. Fucking gentleman you are, I thought to myself while making my way to the bathroom.

"Aubrey?" I heard a voice call. I turned around. Fuck me. The last person I would've wanted to see.

"What are you doing here?" He asked.

"Gee, Josh, I don't know, watching the game?" I responded.

"Don't get snarky with me, Aubrey." I rolled my eyes.

"Okay, have a goodnight, Josh," I said, turning around. He grabbed me by the shoulder and turned me back towards him.

"I wasn't done talking," he said. "Who the fuck are you here with? We both know none of your little girlfriends would've brought you to a damn baseball game. You're seeing someone?"

"We're not together anymore, Josh. Who I see- or don't see- is none of your damn business."

"You bringing some guy around to meet my daughter is sure as hell my business."

"You haven't seen your daughter in two damn years you piece of shit, how the hell do you-" He grabbed my chin roughly, forcing me to look at him. I tried to push him off but he was too strong. I was trapped.

"Watch your mouth you little bitch," he said, tightening his grip around my face.

"What the fuck is going on here?" I recognized the accent right away. Morgan. I couldn't believe he was seeing me like this. I wanted to melt into a puddle. That is so embarrassing. Josh finally let go of me. I rubbed my face slightly, looking down embarrassingly.

"What kind of piece of shit grabs a woman like that?" He said, obviously disdainful of what he had just witnessed.

"Who the fuck are you, cowboy?"

"Aubrey, you okay?" Morgan asked me, ignoring Josh completely.

"Oh, I see what this is. He's the guy you're fucking!" Josh yelled out. "Redneck piece of shit," he mumbled under his breath.

"What did you just call me?" Morgan said, slightly raising his eyebrows as he asked the question.

"I said you were a redneck piece of shit who likes to fuck pathetic single moms cause you can't-" he didn't even get to finish his sentence before Morgan's fist met the side of his nose. Fuck. He fell to the ground almost immediately, holding his bloody nose.

"Wanna say that again?" Morgan said, holding him down by the collar of his shirt.

"Morgan! I'm fine, don't-" I couldn't even finish speaking before I was blinded by the flash of a camera. And another. And another. Morgan grabbed me by the hand, and started walking towards the exit.

"C'mon girl, we gotta go," he said, walking increasingly fast. The cameras were following us through the crowded area.

"What's going on, why are they taking pictures?" I asked, out of breath.

"Oh my god, is that Morgan Wallen?" some girl asked, pointing towards us.

"Morgan! Can I get a picture please?"

He ignored them both, making his way to the parking lot without letting go of my hand. What the hell is happening? Who is this guy? He unlocked his truck and instructed me to get in. I didn't even have time to fasten my seatbelt before he drove off.

I had been quiet for the first few minutes of the drive, trying to silently make sense of what had just happened.

"Who the fuck was that guy anyway?" He asked, pulling me from my thoughts.

"My daughter's dad," I admitted embarrassingly.

"Oh."

"It's fine, he's not a part of her life. Or mine for that matter," I added.

"I see," he said. The question was burning my lips. I had to ask him.

"So, hum, who are you..?" I asked. He chuckled.

"Just some guy who wasn't about to let that asshole put his hands on a pretty girl like you."

"That's not what I meant," I said calmly. "The cameras and the girls asking for pictures... What was that about?"

"I guess you could say I make some music," he said modestly.

"So is this whole altercation going to be all over the internet or something..?" I asked. He chuckled lightly.

"I told you you was gonna be trouble," he said, resting his right hand on my thigh. I felt flutters in my stomach.

"I wasn't trying to-"

"I'm kidding," he said calmly. "You didn't ask me to do that. I got a bit carried away hearing him speak of you like that."

"Thank you," I said.

"What for?"

"Saving me, I guess."

"You don't strike me as the kind of girl who needs to be saved. But glad I could be of service," he said, squeezing my thigh slightly. "So, baby, where do you wanna go?"

Chapter 3

"So, baby, where do you wanna go?" he asked.

"I don't know, maybe we should call Jared to let him know we left," I answered.

"Is that really what you wanna do?" he asked, turning towards me quickly without his hand leaving my thigh. I didn't want Jared to worry, which I knew he would. But I also wanted to get to know Morgan better, whatever that meant, and I knew Jared would not want me to be alone with him.

"Scratch that, let's go have a drink," I said. He smiled without taking his eyes off the road.

"Alright then girl," he said. "So, where to?"

"I know just the place. Make a left at the light."

He pulled into the dusty drive-way of this little barn a couple minutes off the main road. The place was poorly lit by a couple of outdated Christmas lights and a flickering neon sign. I opened the door and jumped out of the lifted truck.

"Where did you get this truck anyway?"

"It's mine."

"You drove here? From Tennessee?!"

"Yeah, better than a crowded plane. It gave me time to think."

"Yeah, I bet a 17 hour drive gave you plenty of time to think," I chuckled.

"Maybe I'll have a reason to do the drive more often now," he said, looking into my eyes. My heart skipped a beat. I broke eye contact, looking down at my feet and smiling timidly.

"Yeah, maybe so," I answered, still avoiding his gaze.

"So, where the hell did you bring me," he asked, scratching the back of his neck while he looked at the old neon sign.

"Somewhere no one will know who you are." I winked at him.

"Okay," he chuckled. "I trust that you won't get me killed," he added, grabbing my hand and intertwining our fingers nonchalantly as we walked through the door. The place hadn't changed at all. The same old steel bar stools were still standing around the wooden bar. A couple of black tables and rusty chairs were available around the two occupied pool tables. The place was big, but had lost its notoriety. A total of ten people, mostly older men, were gathered around the two pool tables, smoking and drinking beer.

"Well ain't that a nice surprise," I heard the lady behind the bar say. I couldn't believe Mama Jo was still standing behind that bar.

"Mama Jo!"

"Please tell me you got rid of that piece of dirt, what was his name?"

"Josh, and yeah, he's long gone," I chuckled and caught Morgan smiling from the corner of my eye.

"Good. Now who's the gentleman?" she asked, pointing to Morgan with her chin.

"Oh that's Morgan," I answered.

"Nice to meet you ma'am."

"Oh please, everybody calls me Mama Jo," she said. "Have you been taking good care of my little Aubrey here?"

"Oh, we're not dating," I said. "We kinda just met actually."

"Well, I know that look when I see it in a man's eye, honey, and that guy is not trying to be 'just a friend'," she said, covering the side of her mouth as though that would make him unable to hear what she was saying. I could feel the temperature rising in my cheeks.

"Can we get two whiskeys?" Morgan asked, saving me from the awkward conversation.

"A man that knows what he wants, I like that. Why don't you two lovebirds go sit down and I'll bring it to you," she said, winking at me. We thanked her and I followed Morgan to the hickory booth in the back corner of the room. I sat across from him.

"She's a lot, I'm sorry," I apologized.

"Hey, anything for a night of privacy," he grinned shyly. "So, where did you find this place?"

"My dad used to take me here when I was little. My mom and I lived in Maine, but every summer she'd ship me off to my dad in Vermont so she could spend the summer on tour with her band."

"She was in a band?" he asked.

"It was more an excuse to get hammered on the road with her friends than it was a band if you ask me, but yeah."

"Oh," he said quietly.

"It's fine. I loved spending my summers with my dad. He'd bring me here and I'd get to play pool with his buddies and sing on the karaoke machine, and Mama Jo would always bring me the crispiest soda," I said, smiling to myself, thinking back upon those memories.

"Two whiskeys for you my darlings," said Mama Jo, pulling me out of my thoughts. "Anything else?" she asked, putting the drinks down on the coasters.

"No, we're good. Thanks Mama Jo," I said. She smiled and walked back to the bar. I felt my phone buzzing against the table. I looked at the screen. Shit.

"It's Jared," I said. Morgan grinned.

"So what are you gonna do?" he laughed, mocking me.

"I don't know? Do I pick up?"

"Girl, you look like a teenager about to get grounded," he chuckled. I didn't even have time to respond before he picked up my phone and put it on speaker.

"Hey Jared," he said. I took a sip of my whiskey. This couldn't be good.

"Morgan? Where are you guys? Is Aubrey okay?"

"I'm fine Jared, we're just... at the park," I said, panicking. Morgan tilted his head, quietly laughing at me. 'The park?' he mouthed silently, confused. I shook my head.

"The park? Which park? I hear music," Jared said.

"Yeah, there's a, um, fiesta at the park. A Mexican fiesta, with tacos and everything," I said, shrugging at Morgan who looked at me even more confused than before.

"Really? Where? We are kind of starving, we'll swing by for some tacos, right guys?" he asked. I heard Ernest and Jesse agreeing in the background. Fuck!!

"They're fully booked now actually, they won't let anyone else in," I said.

"They're fully booked... at the park?" Jared asked, confused.

"Yeah.. Um, the reception is actually quite bad, Jared, I can't hear you well, but thank you for the amazing night and I will text you in the morning! Bye!" I said, grabbing my phone out of Morgan's hands and hanging up. He looked at me and bursted out laughing.

"Girl, you are a terrible liar," he laughed.

"Shut up," I said, flipping him off. "Why did you pick up?"

"Why not? You ain't gotta be scared of fucking Jared," he giggled.

"I'm not scared of him," I said. "You're the one who's scared of him. You said earlier that you would've kissed me if it wasn't for him," I shrugged defensively. He bit his bottom lip slightly and narrowed his eyes.

"Careful, you're on dangerous grounds," he warned.

"Oh yeah? Am I lying though?" I dared. He got up from his side of the booth and came to join me on my side. I slid down the seat and he sat down next to me, trapping me between him and the wall.

"Wanna say that again?" he dared me.

"I think you won't make a move on me 'cause you're scared of Jared," I said without breaking eye contact. He got closer to me, so close I could feel the warmth of his breath tickling my lips. He put a strand of hair behind my left ear softly.

"Definitely not scared," he whispered, locking his lips with mine. He tasted like whiskey and tobacco. His lips were soft and his mustache tickled my nose slightly. He opened his mouth and let his tongue flirt with mine, putting his left hand on the back of my head to deepen the kiss. I could feel his right hand moving slowly from the small of my back to my butt. My heart was racing. Finally. I wrapped my left arm around the back of his neck and moved closer to him. Both of his hands grabbed my hips roughly and he sat me down on top of him. My knees were on the booth and I could feel his jeans rubbing against mine between my legs. Things were getting hot. Too hot. Too fast. I could feel the table digging in my back. I slowly pulled away from the kiss. He looked at me and bit his bottom lip, his hands still on my hips. I put my hands on his shoulders, ensuring a safe distance between our lips. I could feel him getting hard through the fabric of his jeans. Oh my god.

"Are you okay..?" he asked softly. "We don't have to-"

"Do you wanna get out of here?" I asked. He smiled at me. The most handsome, devilish smile I had ever seen.

"Let's go."

I hope you guys like this! Feel free to leave some feedback! xo

Chapter 4 (smut)

✱ **WARNING MATURE/SEXUAL CONTENT** (If you don't like smut you can skip this chapter, the story will still make sense, I promise)

I unlocked the door of my apartment with Morgan's hands on my hips and his mouth on my neck. I could feel his erection pressing against my lower back. Damn keys. "Do you need help?" he murmured in my ear, biting my earlobe slightly. I giggled. "I got it," I said, finally getting the door unlocked. I barely had time to walk in before he pulled on my hips and swung me around so that I was facing him. He paused to look into my eyes. "You're beautiful," he said. "Shh, we can't be loud. The walls are paper thin and my daughter is sleeping next door," I whispered. He smiled. "You're beautiful" he repeated, whispering, without taking his eyes off me. I blushed. He grabbed me by the waist and brought me closer to him. I unconsciously bit my lower lip and he put his thumb on it, freeing it from my teeth. "The things I wanna do to you right now," he murmured. "I want you," I whispered. What the fuck? Why would you say that? He groaned slightly and roughly put his lips on mine. They were warm and soft. I opened my mouth slightly, allowing his tongue to slip inside. He put both of his hands on my ass, bringing me closer in. I could feel how hard he was through the fabric of his jeans. Please take my shirt off already. His hands ran up from my butt all the way to the bottom of my shirt. He stopped there for a minute, pressing his lips harder against mine before breaking the kiss for a second to pass my shirt over my head. Shit, can he hear my thoughts? I looked into his eyes and let my fingers run inside the elastic band of his boxers, playing with it softly. He breathed loudly before taking my fingers off."Not yet, baby", he groaned. What? Why? "Take me to your bed," he whispered into my ear. I grabbed his hand gently, intertwining our fingers, and led him to my bedroom. He put both his thumbs inside the top of my jeans, directing me towards the bed while kissing me softly. I felt the foot of the bed bump into the back of my thighs when he grabbed my legs and sat me down on it without breaking the kiss. He pushed me onto the bed, my back unexpectedly falling flat onto it. I moaned slightly at the surprise. He smiled. He climbed on the bed, pressing his erection into my pelvis, rubbing it against me slightly while maintaining eye contact. His eyes were narrower than they were before. His gaze felt burning hot on me. He gave me a peck on the lips and his hands brushed over my naked breasts, going all the way down the button of my jeans, which he undid quickly. He looked into my eyes, as if he was seeking my permission to go further. I nodded slightly and he began to kiss my lower stomach softly, unzipping my pants and trailing the kisses further down. He grabbed both my jeans and underwear and took them off at once. I suddenly felt so naked. Shy almost. But it was only a second before he went back to kissing my lower stomach teasingly. Holy shit, is he going to eat me ou- I couldn't finish that thought before his lips landed on my pussy, kissing it softly, slowly licking up and down my clit. I tried to suppress a moan, in vain, and felt him smile against me. I could feel my vagina pulsing already. His tongue was sliding up and down my -wet- pussy, his lips suctioning lightly around my clit. I put my right hand over my mouth, trying to keep the noises in, while the fingers of my other hand were running through his hair, pulling it lightly as the pleasure was overcoming me. I felt him pull away for a second and put a finger in his mouth. The same finger that was inside me seconds later, hitting exactly the right spot. He put his mouth back on my clit while adding a second finger and sliding them in and out of me slowly. I could feel the electricity coursing through my veins. I closed my eyes and involuntarily whimpered. "Oh my god, I'm gonna cum," I panted. He stopped and smirked. "Not yet," he said, pulling his fingers out of me and undoing his belt. I shivered in excitement. "You still want me, baby?" he asked, looking in my eyes to make sure. I nodded frantically. He took off his belt and unbuttoned his jeans, taking them off along with his boxers. Oh my god. That's a lot bigger than Josh's. He wrapped his right hand around the base of his cock and rubbed it against my wet, puffy pussy lips, before slowly sliding it in. "Fuck," he groaned, pushing it all the way in. I gasped. It was big. It felt big. It felt... good. Really good. He grabbed my hips, bringing me closer to him to get a better angle and I wrapped my legs around him, allowing him to go even deeper inside me. I squeaked, instantly covering my mouth."You feel so fucking good baby," he panted, thrusting into me. "Don't you dare cover that mouth, I wanna hear all of your pretty little noises," he groaned, hitting his hips against mine roughly. I let out a needy moan."That's it," he whispered, locking his lips with mine. He pulled my hips down harder, setting a rhythm that was hitting that sinful spot with every thrust. I dug my fingernails into his back, wrapping my legs tighter around his waist. I could feel the pressure of an orgasm building into my lower abdomen. I moaned softly."Are you gonna cum, baby," he whispered into my ear, probably feeling my pussy pulsing around his cock. I moaned again, unable to get words out. He grinned, hitting my g-spot harder."Oh my god, Morgan, I"m gonna c-" I couldn't finish my sentence before shockwaves coursed through my entire body. It was like the earth had stopped spinning on its axis. In this moment, nothing mattered but him and I and our bodies becoming one. He grabbed my waist and started pounding his hips harder into me. His rhythm was starting to be off and he had trouble focusing. I knew he was gonna cum soon."Don't cum insi-"He groaned and stopped thrusting, his dick throbbing deep inside my pussy. I felt the thick, hot cum drooling inside me. Fuck. He pulled out, laying down next to me to catch his breath. "What were you saying?" he panted. "Nothing," I answered. He turned his head towards me, looking to see if there was something wrong. I smiled faintly. He smiled back. "Come here," he said, pulling me into his chest and kissing the top of my head. I nuzzled up against him and he rubbed my back softly. I could've stayed like that forever. I closed my eyes and without even noticing it fell asleep, on his chest, right then and there.

Chapter 5

I opened my eyes to the sound of my daughter crying through the wall. I looked at the clock on my nightstand. 6:14 AM. Ms. Brown told Jared to come by at 9, right? I can stay in bed a little while longer. I turned around to make sure Morgan was still in bed and found him sleeping peacefully next to me. I smiled to myself. That was a good night. After 3 years of celibacy, I deserved this, no? I closed my eyes for a split second before hearing my phone buzzing against the nightstand. I grabbed it and looked at the screen.

CHELSEA 6:16 AM

Aubrey, is that you??? *hyperlink*

Shit. I clicked on the link, already knowing all too well what it would be about. An article titled "Morgan Wallen Gets Into Physical Altercation with Fan and Flees the Scene with Mystery Girl", accompanied by a picture of Morgan holding Josh down by the collar of his shirt, and one of him and I walking hand in hand towards the parking lot, popped up on the screen. Shit. I put my phone back on the nightstand and turned towards Morgan who was awake, looking at me. I jumped and he chuckled.

"Sorry, I didn't mean to startle you," he said.

"That's okay," I smiled faintly. He looked into my eyes and put the strand of hair that was falling in my face behind my ear.

"You're even prettier in the morning," he whispered. I blushed, breaking eye contact. "You'll have to work on accepting compliments 'cause that ain't gonna stop," he chuckled, grazing my face with his fingertips. I smiled and he pulled me in closer, kissing my forehead. I sighed.

"Are you okay, baby?"

I paused to think. "I guess so," I responded, subconsciously biting on my fingernail.

"What's up? You can tell me," he said, his fingertips still gently stroking the side of my face.

"Someone put out an article with pictures of what happened last night," I mumbled. He rubbed his eyebrows with his index and his thumb, like he was trying to make sense of what I had just said.

"What did it say?" he asked. I grabbed my phone and showed him the article. He sighed, throwing it lightly on the bed. "Fuck. I gotta call my manager," he said, quickly getting out of bed, still naked, and grabbing his clothes and his phone. "Bathroom?" he asked.

"First door on the left." He nodded and left the room. I sighed. Should I have not said anything? I grabbed my phone that was still in the bed and replied to Chelsea.

AUBREY 6:27 AM

Hey Chels, yeah, that's me. Long story.

CHELSEA 6:28 AM

You know Morgan Wallen? And is that Josh??

Fuck. Chelsea had been my best friend since elementary school. She knew my entire life story and I knew hers. We'd been with each other through thick and thin and, while she was still living in Maine, we would make arrangements to see each other every couple of months and spoke on the phone every week. I loved her to death, but I did not want to get into specifics right now.

AUBREY 6:30 AM

Yeah, he's a friend of Jared's. You know him?

AUBREY 6:30 AM

Also, yes that's Josh.....

CHELSEA 6:31 AM

What do you mean 'do I know him'?? Everybody knows him, Aubrey, he's freaking Morgan Wallen!! *screenshot*

CHELSEA 6:32 AM

Careful though, I heard he's kind of a dick :/

I looked at the picture she'd sent me. It was a screenshot of Billboard Hot 100 where his name comfortably sat at no 1. They even had his picture up. God he's hot- Not the point, Aubrey, focus. I could not believe he was that famous. Had I been living under a rock? And why did she say he was a dick? I needed to figure this guy out.

AUBREY 6:34 AM

I'll call you later, Chels. Thanks for the info! x

I opened google and typed in his name. Let's find out who you are, Morgan Wallen. A ton of pictures popped up. Links to his spotify, youtube, instagram, wikipedia page, but I needed to dig a little bit deeper than the surface. Then came the articles. "Morgan Wallen Gets Kicked Out of Kid Rock's Bar and Arrested" "Morgan Wallen Caught Making Out with Every Alabama Sorority Girl During Lockdown" What the fuck? I clicked on the link and a video started playing immediately. I turned the sound off so that he couldn't hear it from the bathroom. We could clearly see him, visibly drunk, making out with a first girl, grabbing a second girl's ass, making out with a third girl. And a fourth. And a fifth. I felt my heart sink into my stomach. How could I have been this stupid. I deleted the page and my search history and put my phone back on my nightstand. I got out of bed and got dressed immediately, suddenly feeling incredibly aware of how naked I was. I put my hair in a simple ponytail and I heard him come out of the bathroom.

"So I spoke with my manager, he's gonna have a talk with my PR rep and figure out the best way to approach this," he said, walking towards my bedroom. He walked in and looked at me.

"Well, aren't you pretty, all dressed up," he said, putting his hands on my hips. I took a step back. He furrowed his eyebrows, visibly confused.

"Everything okay..?"

"Yeah, I'm fine. I should probably go get my daughter," I mumbled, avoiding eye contact.

"Right now? It's not even 7:00 AM yet, I thought Jared said-"

"Well, Jared isn't in charge, I am," I answered dryly.

"Okay..? Can we at least get coffee..?" he asked tentatively.

"I'm not sure that would be a good idea."

"I don't understand wh-"

"Look, we made a mistake, we shouldn't have. Let's not complicate things," I said.

"A mistake? Baby, don't say it like that," he said, taking a step towards me, putting his hands on my hips again. I looked down, staring at his boots, avoiding eye contact at all cost, but he lifted my chin with his two fingers and looked into my eyes. His eyes felt sincere, that was the worst part. He didn't look like an asshole, but I still couldn't shake the image of him making out with a

million different girls in the span of a single night. And that's just the time he got caught. I shivered.

"Are you cold?" he asked.

"I'm fine."

"Do you want me to leave..?" he asked. I didn't get to answer before I heard a knock on the door.

"Who the hell knocks on people's doors at 7:00 freaking AM", I mumbled, making my way towards the door with Morgan following suit. I swung the door open only to discover Jared standing on the other side. Shit. He looked at me quietly, then looked at Morgan, and back at me. He chuckled dryly.

"I see what this is," he said.

"Jared it's not-" I began. He turned away from me and looked straight into Morgan's eyes, pointing his finger at him.

"You. You could've had any girl last night. Why the fuck would you do this?! Fucking friend you are," he snarled. He looked at me.

"And you," he scoffed. "Congrats on being the 10 000th girl to fuck Morgan Wallen, Aubrey", he spat before turning around shaking his head and disappearing down the stairs. I was speechless. In the span of one night, I had managed to piss off one of my best friends and have sex -for the first time in three damn years- with someone who fucks one girl after the other. Nice going, Aubrey. I sighed and closed the door.

"What do we do now?" Morgan asked.

"What do you mean 'what do we do now'?! You go home and keep singing your songs and making out with random girls and I'll try and fix the friendship I just ruined for no good reason," I snapped.

"That's not fair."

"Well, life ain't fair, you'll be fine," I responded dryly.

"It's not like I twisted your arm, you were coming onto me," he said nonchalantly. Wow. Who the fuck does this guy think he is. I could feel my blood boiling.

"Yeah, I bet those sorority sisters were coming onto you too," I said. His eyes widened.

"Is that what this is about?! Something I did three fucking years ago? That's why you're so mad right now?" he said. Shit. "And how the hell do you even know about that? You said you didn't know me. What, you lied?"

"No, I-"

"That's fucked up-"

"I didn't lie!" I yelled. "My friend saw the pictures of you and I and she texted me saying you were kind of a dick so I googled you," I admitted, semi-embarrassed.

"Ah, Google. The best way to get to know someone for who they truly are," he snapped sarcastically.

"You know what, screw you. I know exactly what kind of guy you are. Love 'em and leave 'em, am I right? Well, I don't deserve this. I deserve someone great. Someone who likes me!"

"You do," he said.

"Exactly!"

"Exactly! So why are we fighting?" he rejoined.

"I don't know!" I snapped back. I didn't even have time to think before he grabbed my face and kissed me roughly. He let his fingers run into my hair and pushed me slightly. Our bodies pressed together heatedly against the wall, breathing heavily as our lips danced together. I could feel the soft tickle of his breath beneath my nose. What are you doing, Aubrey? I pulled away.

"I'm not just another one of these girls you can just shut up with a kiss!" I defended myself.

"I don't think that! I just... wanted to kiss you," he retorted softly.

"Yeah, well, you want to kiss a lot of people. And I slept with you, are you even clean?"

"Aubrey! Yes, I'm clean! And just 'cause I like to make out with pretty girls every once in a while doesn't mean I sleep with all of them!" I rolled my eyes. "It's true!" he continued. "Look, I like that you're hard working and that you stand up for yourself. I like that you're a mom and that you take your responsibilities to heart, I like you. Please don't make this out to be something it's not," he said, almost pleading. He seemed genuine, but I still wanted to be careful. I didn't have the luxury to bring just anyone in my life. I had to protect my daughter and be cautious of the people she got attached to. With everything that had happened with her dad, I couldn't afford to drag her along another failed relationship. And I still couldn't shake what I had seen, or what Jared had said.

"It just sucks to feel like just any girl could have been in bed with you last night. Like it didn't have to be me. But, we didn't make each other any promises, Morgan. You did nothing wrong. I just got a bit carried away. It's fine."

"Well, that's simply not true-"

"I think you should go."

I hope you guys like this! Feel free to give feedback, always

XO

LadyBug

Chapter 6

A couple of days had passed since I had last seen Morgan. I was back at work, and Jared was still not talking to me. I was sitting at my desk, waiting for the day to go by, hoping that we could go back to our usual banter, but doubtful that it would happen. My days felt dull without him. I missed my friend.

"When is my next patient?" He asked, startling me.

"10 minutes," I mumbled. "Jared, can we talk?" I asked, turning towards him.

"Thanks," he answered dryly, his eyes not leaving his clipboard. He turned around and left the reception to go back to his office. I sighed. My heart had felt heavy every time I had seen him over the last couple of days. I knew I would disappoint him by leaving with Morgan. I knew he'd be hurt and I had still done it. I deserve the cold shoulder. The phone rang, pulling me out of my thoughts.

"Lakeside Medical Center, how can I help you?"

"Um, yeah, Aubrey please," the voice said. I froze, recognizing who it belonged to instantly.

"This is she, how can I help you?"

"Hi, it's Morgan... um Wallen-"

"Yep, figured with the first name," I said dryly.

"Can we talk?" he asked. I noticed Jared was back, looking at charts behind me.

"Would you like to make an appointment, sir?" I asked formally.

"Uh, not really, I was really just hoping to talk to you."

"Unfortunately Dr. Munsen is fully booked this week, but I might be able to squeeze you in with someone else, if you'd like," I said.

"Please call me when you get home... Uh, this is my phone number, maybe write it down. Please don't give it to anyone, not that I think you would, but uh-" I rolled my eyes.

"Maybe try going to the bathroom, sir. Maybe that could help you not feel so full." of yourself, you dick. He chuckled.

"Alright, it's 865-351-6290, please call me Aubrey, we need to talk," he said ominously before hanging up.

What the hell was that about it? I grabbed my cell phone right away, unable to wait until the end of the day to give him a piece of my mind.

AUBREY 4:28

Do not call me at work!! That is incredibly unprofessional!!

MORGAN 4:29

I don't have to be professional, I don't work there ;)

Cocky piece of shit.

AUBREY 4:30

Don't. Call. My. Work. Period. And don't call me at all for that matter.

I shoved my phone back in my purse and went back to work.

"Personal emergency?" Jared asked. I jumped.

"Hardly."

"You can't use your phone at work unless it's an emergency," he snapped, grabbing a file from my desk and going back to his office. I sighed.

"What is up with you two?" Amy asked. She was the other secretary at the clinic. A nice girl from Texas, in her late twenties, whom I always thought had a bit of a thing for Jared. She had long brown hair and dark eyes. Her skin had a nice little tan to it, like she had just gotten back from a week in Mexico. She had been working at the clinic long before I got here. I don't think she liked me much at first, but we had grown accustomed to one another and she would never pass on an opportunity to gossip with me.

"I fucked up," I admitted. She raised an eyebrow in a 'tell me more' kind of fashion.

"He brought me to a baseball game last week so that I could meet his friends, and I kind of hit it off with one of them."

"Oh, that's rough," she said. "Which friend?"

"You know them..?" I asked.

"One of them came by, a couple years back, asking to see Dr. Munsen. I can't remember his name but he was tall, brown haired and covered in tattoos, kind of good looking," she said.

"Jesse?" I offered.

"Yeah, Jesse! That's it! Well, Jesse had blood all over his shirt and was in quite rough shape. Dr. Munsen saw him right away and asked me to cancel his afternoon. I swear to god they spent the whole day in that office and did not come out until after I had gone home. It was the weirdest thing," she said. That is weird. I guess Jared too had some secrets after all.

"Yeah, weird," I pondered. "I met Jesse, but no, it wasn't him."

"Oh, well then I probably don't know him, I don't think I've met any his other friends," she said.

"His name is Morgan. If he calls here asking for me, just do me a favor and tell him I'm not in."

"Alright, will do," she smiled. I gave her a faint smile back and looked at the time on my computer. 5:00 PM.

"Alright, I'm out of here, I'll see you tomorrow," I said, grabbing my purse from under my desk.

"See you tomorrow, Aubrey!"

***

I opened the fridge, scratching the back of my head.

"What do you want for dinner, Ellie?" I asked my three year old daughter.

"Mac and cheese!" she yelled.

"El, we can't have mac and cheese everyday, it's not good for you."

"I want mac and cheese!" she screamed, stomping her foot. I knew she was just exhausted from going to daycare and playing outside all day, but my patience was wearing thin after the day I had had.

"Ellie, you need to have veggies, and protein if you want to grow strong and tall."

"I want mac and cheese!" she cried, "Mac and cheese, mama! Mac and cheese!"

I heard a knock on the door, barely audible under Ellie's cries and looked through the peephole to see who it was. I saw Glenda Brown standing casually on my doorstep and opened up right away.

"Hi Ms. Brown," I greeted.

"Hi darling, little Ellie seems to be in a bit of a mood. I'll take her for dinner if you want so you can relax a little bit. I've noticed she's been a bit more difficult lately and I know how hard you work," she offered. That woman was truly a godsend.

"You don't have to do that Ms. Brown, I-"

"I insist, darling. It takes a village," she smiled.

"Thank you, I don't know how I will ever repay you for all that you do for us," I said, truly moved by her kindness.

"Oh nonsense. You pay me back everyday by being the cutest little neighbor an old lady like me could've asked for," she told Ellie. "Now come on little Ellie, Ms Glenda has nice hot lasagna in the oven for you," she added, grabbing Ellie by the hand and taking her next door. I closed the door, eternally grateful for the literal angel that woman was. I headed to the bathroom and drew myself a warm bath.

The feeling of the hot water against my skin felt nice. It was like I could finally breathe. Ellie was safely eating next door, I was done with work for the day, everything seemed to be falling into place; at least for today. I took a deep breath in and slowly exhaled, letting all the tension exit my body at once. I lowered my shoulders into the water and closed my eyes.

I got pulled out of my relaxation state a few seconds later by my phone buzzing against the ceramic tiles next to the bathtub. I touched the floor repeatedly without opening my eyes, before finally locating my phone and answering it right away.

"Hello" I said cheerfully, feeling close to fully relaxed by now.

"Hey, I took it upon myself to call you back since you weren't calling," the voice said. I opened my eyes instantly.

"Well, patience is a virtue Mr. Wallen," I answered. He chuckled.

"A virtue that I don't have Ms. Farrell. What are you up to?" he asked. I looked down at my naked body in the water.

"Taking a bath."

"Mmm, yeah baby?"

"Ew, not like that," I said dryly. He laughed. "What do you want, Morgan?"

"I would like for us to actually speak face to face."

"Why?"

"Because there's some things I need to discuss with you," he said in a serious tone.

"And that can't be done over the phone?"

"I'd rather not. I'm in Vermont until tomorrow. Can I swing by your place, maybe tonight?" he asked. I sighed.

"If you have to..."

"Great, I'll be there in 20."

"Wait, give me a few-" I didn't get to finish speaking that he'd already hung up. Ugh.

Chapter 7

I barely had time to get out of the bathtub and get dressed before I heard the knock at my door. I swung the door open.

"Jeez, I thought you said 20 min- Oh, sorry Ms. Brown, hi!"

"Oh, are you expecting someone?" she asked. "Is it the hot doctor?" she whispered, winking at me.

"No, unfortunately not," I chuckled, semi-disappointed myself.

"Well, mind you, our little Ellie fell asleep on the couch watching her cartoons. I can wake her up if you want, but I truly wouldn't mind keeping her for the night. I could even walk her to daycare in the morning if you'd like," she offered.

"You truly are an angel among men Ms. Brown," I said, eternally grateful.

'It really is my pleasure, Aubrey. You know, my kids don't visit me much. Little Ellie is one of the greatest joys of my life."

"Thank you, Ms. Brown, this really means a lot," I thanked her.

"Alright, darling. I'll leave you to it. And sleep in a little later tomorrow if you can, I'll take care of Ellie, you look tired, honey," she said, waving her hand at me and heading back to her apartment. I heard her lock her door and was about to close mine as well when a hand stopped it.

"Hey," Morgan said, opening the door himself.

"Hey?" I answered, baffled by his manners. "Would you like a key as well next time?" he chuckled.

"I mean, if you're offering," he said. I rolled my eyes.

"So, what did you want to talk about?"

"I don't get a drink this time?"

"Boy, who raised you? Wolves?" I snapped. He chuckled.

"I won't tell my mama you just spoke like this of her favorite son," he said jokingly. I forced a smile. "I want you to come on tour with me," he said. I coughed, choking on my own saliva.

"Are you insane?!"

"I'm serious," he retorted.

"So am I! Are you sane? Should you even be driving? What the fuck is wrong with you?" I questioned. He laughed.

"Look, you think I'm a piece of shit, right? You think I'm an asshole who doesn't care about you and your feelings and that you're just one of many names I get to write down in my playbook. Right?"

"You have a playbook? Wow, that's even worse."

"I don't have a playb- Girl, you play too much," he said. I giggled. "I want to prove to you that I am for real. I like you for you. Come on tour with me, I'll show you firsthand that you can trust me. No other girl, no dumb shit, just you and me, girl," he said, looking deep into my eyes. And for a second, I really thought about it. What would it be like to actually go out and see the world with him? Ever since I had had Ellie, I hadn't really done anything crazy. I hadn't left Vermont, or partied (except maybe the few too many whiskeys I'd shared with Morgan that night), or even gone to a single concert. My days were like one big blob of medical files and diaper changes. For a second, I wanted to forget I had responsibilities. I wanted to, but I couldn't.

"I can't, Morgan. You know that," I shook my head.

"Why?"

"Because!" I said. He raised an eyebrow, encouraging me to elaborate. "My daughter, my job, I have a life here. I can't just go on tour with you and leave everything behind. I'm not free like you," I said, defeated.

"My mom can look after your daughter, I already asked her. She looks after my son quite a bit, she was a foster mom, she's great with kids," he stated, making his case. "And your job? C'mon Aubrey, you know Jared would let you off the hook."

"I don't think you know Jared like I do. Plus, he's not even talking to me right now, thanks to you."

"I will fix that. I'll talk to him. Please, let me fix that," he pleaded. He took both my hands in his and looked deep into my eyes. His eyes looked beautiful as ever. And for once, he looked like a real, genuine person. I realized that up until that moment, what I'd seen was a character; a version of him that he chose to present to the world to protect himself. For the first time since I had looked him up online, I started thinking that he might be telling the truth. His eyes were screaming that he cared about me and I wanted to believe him.

"I don't know your mom," I mumbled.

"Come to Tennessee with me tomorrow. I have a whole week left before leaving again to go on tour. You'll meet her and if you don't love her and don't feel comfortable leaving Ellie with her, I'll never mention it again. I'll disappear and I'll leave you alone. I swear," he pleaded. This was crazy. I couldn't possibly think of doing this. But even though my rational side was begging me to tell him no and ask him to leave, the romantic in me actually wanted to give this a shot.

"How long would we be gone?" I asked.

"3 months."

"That's crazy, Morgan. I can't leave my daughter for 3 months. I'd miss her way too much, that's not possible-"

"So we'll fly her in every two weeks, she can watch the show, my mom can even bring Indie along so she'll have a little friend-"

"Indie?"

"Indigo, my son. We can make this work, and when you miss her too much I'll fly you out to Tennessee so you can spend time with her," he explained. He had really thought this through.

"I can't afford that."

"Aubrey," he said, pulling me in a little closer. "Money is the last thing on my mind and it should be the last thing on yours. I will never ask you for a penny, I will pay your rent while you're out there with me, and all of your bills, and anything you want, girl. Please don't let this be an issue."

I wanted to say no. I wanted to call him an overconfident asshole and be the -probably- first girl to ever turn him down and walk away. I wanted to, but before I could even think of what to say, I heard myself answer out loud.

"Fine," I mumbled. His eyes widened and a large grin appeared on his face. He looked like a kid in a candy store.

"Really?!" he asked. I nodded yes. "Baby, baby, baby. I promise you won't regret this."

"You have to speak to Jared though," I said.

"I will go see him right now. Right this minute," he said, opening the door. "Pack your bags baby, you're going to Tennessee."

This is a bit shorter than usual but I hope y'all like it. If you guys liked this chapter, please feel free to leave a comment or give a vote! Any bit of feedback is super appreciated. I hope you guys enjoy reading this as much as I enjoy writing it!

xo

LadyBug

Chapter 8

Morgan hadn't stopped texting me since he had left my apartment. I had packed everything. From clothes, to make up, to diapers and toys, I had everything ready. But the more I looked at my bags, the more I started to panic. I can't do this! This is crazy! I can't let a woman I don't even know take care of Ellie. And I can't leave Jared, especially to go with Morgan. He'll never forgive me. I have to make things right with him before anything else. And Ms. Brown would be so sad if Ellie and I left, I couldn't do that to her. The more time I spent thinking about it, the crazier the idea started to feel. I needed to sleep but my mind wouldn't stop. I had been staring at the ceiling for three hours when my phone buzzed, again, on my nightstand.

MORGAN 1:36 AM

Spoke w/ Jared, everything's okay. You'll still have a job when u get back. I'll pick you and Ellie up at 11 AM, be ready <3

I set my phone down, and went back to staring at the ceiling.

***

I opened my eyes and looked at the clock on my nightstand. 7:00 AM. Solid 30 minutes of sleep. I got up and got dressed for work, unable to actually get ready to leave everything behind. I saw Ms. Brown walking up the stairs as I was getting down, probably on her way back from dropping Ellie off at daycare.

"Hi Ms. Brown," I smiled.

"Oh, hi darling, how are you this morning?"

"I'm okay, I guess."

"I saw the gentleman leaving your apartment last night. That is a good looking man," she giggled.

"Ms. Brown!" I said, putting a hand on my chest, mockingly pretending to be offended. She laughed.

"What's an old lady like me to do if not take a peep!" We both laughed.

"He wants me to follow him to Tennessee for three months," I admitted, secretly fishing for advice.

"Oh darling, how exciting!" she said, to my surprise.

"You wouldn't be upset if Ellie and I left?"

"Upset? For what, honey? I can't be mad at you for living your life! Life is full of little adventures and I've had mine already. But I will miss you, that is, if you decide to leave. Hopefully you still come by and knock on my door every once in a while," she said, pinching my cheek lightly.

"You truly are the sweetest woman to ever walk the earth," I said, pulling her in for a hug.

"You deserve everything that life has to offer, Aubrey. It's not everyday that God sends you someone who makes your heart beat a little faster. Be happy, my darling."

I thanked her and smiled to myself as I made my way towards my car. I kept thinking about what she'd said while I drove to the clinic. What if she was right? What if by not going I would miss out on an incredible life experience. But what if she's wrong. My life is good. I like my life. I like working with Jared, and spending my weekends with Ellie. I like being a hands-on mom and being self-sufficient. I can't just give up my independence to follow someone I barely know.

I pulled into the clinic's parking lot and headed inside. I bumped into Jared on my way in.

"Hey," he said.

"Hey," I mumbled.

"So, you and Morgan huh?"

"I don't know, Jared. Honestly, I don't know."

"He said you were going on tour with him."

"I'm not sure anymore," I admitted.

"I don't think I should weigh in on this. Either way you'll think I'm trying to steal your freedom, or screw Morgan over."

"So, you don't think I should go," I concluded.

"I didn't say that, I'm not saying anything."

"Jared, you're one of the people who knows me best. I trust your judgment. Help me out here?" I begged.

"Why should I, Brey? I trusted you, I really did. I introduced you to my friends because I wanted you to understand me better. To see where I came from. And look where that got me. You don't want to take my advice," he chuckles dryly. "Excuse me," he said, walking past me. I sighed. There was no way I could leave now. No way I could leave things like that between Jared and I. My phone buzzed in my pocket for what felt like the 100th time since last night.

MORGAN 7:58 AM

Baby, is everything okay..?

Shit. I couldn't keep on ignoring his texts, I had to tell him the truth.

AUBREY 8:00 AM

I can't do it, I'm sorry

MORGAN 8:00 AM

Please don't do this.. I already told my mom, she's so excited to meet you, and Ellie...

My heart sank reading that. I didn't want to hurt him. That was the truth. The way he'd spoken to me the night before had changed my perception of him. I genuinely thought he was a good person deep down, and the last thing I wanted was to leave him high and dry, but I couldn't just uproot my life like that. I couldn't leave things the way they were with Jared. After everything he'd done for me, sticking by me through thick and thin, I couldn't just desert him like that. I had more honor than that.

AUBREY 8:03 AM

I'm sorry, just forget about me.

"An emergency?" Jared asked, standing behind me, ready to tell me to put my phone away.

"I just told Morgan I wouldn't go with him," I admitted.

"Oh," he said. "Because of me..?" he asked.

"And other things."

"Don't stop yourself on my account," he said coldly.

"Jared..."

"What?"

"I fucked up, I know I did. But, c'mon... What can I do to make things go back to the way they were? I don't want to lose you over this. You're way more important than any other guy to me."

He sighed, scratching the back of his head.

"You hurt me, Brey. I want us to go back to being friends, but you can't ask me to just forget that anything ever happened. I wish I could, I do. But things just don't work like that. But I forgive you, if that means anything. I'm not mad at you, you're fine."

"I respect that, I'll do what I can to gain your trust back. You don't have to worry about me running away with your friend, that won't happen," I assured him. He smiled at me.

"Alright, get to work Ms. Farrell," he said jokingly.

***

I put Ellie to bed and turned my phone back on. 8 missed calls, all from Morgan. I knew I had gotten his hopes up and let him down. The thought of him being disappointed in me made me sick. I genuinely felt like we had had a connection that night. Even Mama Jo seemed to think so.

He was the first person I'd brought to Kemp's Dive Bar since my dad had passed. I wanted to see where things could go between us, but I couldn't do it to other people's expense. My phone rang. I picked up, already knowing who it was.

"Hello?"

"Please change your mind," he said, audibly hurt.

"Morgan, I can't. I-"

"You know what sucks, Aubrey? It's that when we first met you actually liked me. We genuinely hit it off at that game and we had an awesome night and amazing sex and then you took it upon yourself to google me and that ruined everything. It's always the same thing. Whenever I meet a girl that I actually like and think 'If all goes well, there's a very real possibility that this lady could be my wife someday', everytime it goes back to this. She's either in it for the money, or the fame, or even just to tell her dumb friends that she fucked Morgan Wallen as if that would get her bonus points or something. And with you it was actually different. You had no idea who I was and for a minute there I really thought you wouldn't care. But, you'd rather believe everyone's two cents about me, people that have never even met me. You'd rather believe that than to actually get to know me. Yeah I fucked up a couple times, and yeah there's a whole bunch of tiktoks of me drunk off my ass, making out with a dozen Alabama sorority girls, but did you even bother to ask me what happened? No, of course not. You don't care what let me there, you don't care about me, just care about what other people think of me. You're just like the rest of them," He snapped before hanging up. I sat there, looking at my phone, hoping he would call back, but he didn't. I should have listened to Ms. Brown. My hands were shaking and I felt like I was about to throw up. He was right. The minute I had seen what strangers were saying about him I had stopped giving him the benefit of the doubt. As if he wasn't a real person, with real feeling, that could potentially feel hurt by my actions. I couldn't stop thinking about what he had said about seeing me as a potential wife. The worst part was that I felt that way about him too. I wished I'd never looked him up. I'd give anything to go back to that night. Why did I have to go and complicate things... I felt a warm tear roll down my left cheek. C'mon, Aubrey, don't fucking cry. I took a deep breath in and exhaled slowly, trying to regulate my emotions. I fucked everything up. He really isn't coming back this time.

Thank you to everyone who took the time to vote and comment! You have no idea how happy it makes me to see that some of you genuinely like this story! Hopefully you like this update!

xo

LadyBug

Chapter 9

I got to work the next day and Jared was waiting for me next to my desk.

"Hey," I mumbled.

"You're late," he said.

"I know, I'm sorry, I couldn't sleep last night-"

"I don't need to hear any excuses from you, you're fired."

"What?! Jared, are you serious?! I am 6 minutes late! You're seriously going to fire me over 6 minutes?!"

He grinned.

"Look on your desk," he said, pointing to a piece of paper he had printed out.

"What's this?" I asked.

"Read it," he ordered. I grabbed the piece of paper and brought it closer to my face, slightly unsure of what was going on.

"Plane tickets? Why?"

"I spoke with Morgan last night. I know you're only staying here because of me. Look, I know you're afraid that our friendship will be ruined if you leave, but I'm telling you; it'll be fine," he said, seemingly genuine. "You're my best friend, Aubrey. I know you like him and I know he likes you and I don't want to stand in the way of that. So, you go and see if that's truly the life you want because if you don't you'll end up resenting me and I don't want that."

"I won't resent you," I mumbled.

"I don't want to stand in the way of your happiness. Or even his for that matter. I know everything you've been through in the last couple of years and you deserve the break. You should get to be happy. Even if it doesn't involve me," he said looking down.

"I'm happy here," I stated.

"So, you want me to get a refund on the tickets or...?"

"No," I admitted.

"Now let me give you some eye drops, you look like you cried all night," he said, pulling out a small vial from the cabinet behind us. I looked down, slightly embarrassed he had noticed.

"So, why are you firing me? I was kinda hoping I could get my job back when I'd come home."

"The severance package," he whispered, winking at me.

"Oh, Jared you don't have to-"

"I want to. Morgan mentioned how you didn't want to give up your financial independence and I totally get that, you shouldn't have to. And you won't. Or at least, not for a little while," he smiled. I didn't know what to say. I knew Jared well and his pride often got in the way of things. For him to come out and do this for me meant a lot. I knew he didn't want me to leave. I knew he probably was still wary of Morgan and would have preferred if I stayed here, in Vermont, with him. But he still made the arrangements for me to go and do my thing. He wanted me to be happy and he chose my happiness over his own. Not a lot of people would've done that, even for a friend.

"I don't know what to say, Jared."

"Then don't say anything. No goodbyes, no tears. Go get Ellie and head to the airport, your plane leaves at 12."

"Jared, I-"

"Go! Before I change my mind," he teased. I smiled at him.

"Okay," I whispered, swallowing back tears of joy. "Thank you, Jared," I said as I walked away.

***

I got home and grabbed the bags I had packed the night before. I was ready to go pack the car when I checked my phone. No texts. No missed calls. Nothing. What if he doesn't want me to come anymore? I decided to call him before making any drastic move. It rang twice before he picked up.

"Aubrey?"

"Hey, um, am I bugging you?"

"Not really, what's up?," he asked. I heard a girl giggle in the background and my heart sank.

"Um, you must be home by now."

"I am, why?"

"Who are you with?"

"Like that's any of your business," he said dryly.

"You're right, nevermind I shouldn't have called, I-"

"My sister," he interrupted. "I'm with my sister, Ashlyne."

"Oh."

"What do you want, Aubrey? Besides to monitor who can and can't spend time with apparently."

"Do you still want me to go on tour with you...?" I asked, almost embarrassed by my question. He didn't answer right away. The line went silent for a while, almost as if he was pondering.

"Why?" he finally asked. "It's not like you actually want to come so why mess with me like that?"

"Jared bought plane tickets for Ellie and I," I admitted. "We squashed whatever that was and if you'll still have us, we would love to come see you."

"Are you for real this time?" he said, still unsure of whether or not I was messing with him.

"That would be a bit of a cruel joke, don't you think?" I giggled. He sighed and I swear to god I could hear a smile in that sigh.

"What time do you land? I'll have someone pick you up."

***

We landed in Knoxville at 11 o'clock at night after two flights and a 6 hour layover in Washington. Ellie was exhausted and so was I. I had spoken on the phone with Morgan during the layover and he had assured me that there would be a driver waiting for us as soon as we got off the plane to get us to his parent's house in Sneedville. I got my bags from the baggage claim and looked for the driver. There were a couple of them, each holding a sign with their client's name on it. I scanned the room looking for our sign and finally found it. I rolled my eyes. Mrs. Aubrey Wallen & Ms. Ellie. I waved at the driver who immediately came to help me with the bags.

"I'm guessing you're Mrs. Wallen and this must be Ms. Ellie," the driver said, shaking my daughter's hand.

"I like your hat," she said.

"And I like your shoes," he answered, looking at her little glow in the dark Frozen sneakers. She giggled. "My name is Andrew, and I will be driving you out to Sneedville tonight. It will be about a 90 minute drive, and Mr. Wallen has requested some snacks for Ms. Ellie and champagne for you Mrs. Wallen. If you have any other requests or would like me to make an extra stop, don't be shy, I am at your disposal," he added formally while carrying our luggage towards the car.

"Thank you, Andrew, that is very nice of you. Unnecessary, but very kind," I smiled. "Also, please call me Aubrey because if I hear you call me Mrs. Wallen one more time my head might explode," I joked. Ellie giggled.

"Very well, Aubrey," he answered, opening the door for Ellie and I to get in the car. And of course, the minute I got in the car I noticed a bottle of Dom Perignon in an ice bucket along with a whole bunch of snacks for Ellie. I took a picture of the bottle and sent it to Morgan.

MORGAN 11:37 PM

?

AUBREY 11:38 PM

THAT IS A 300$ BOTTLE OF CHAMPAGNE, SIR

MORGAN 11:40 PM

345 actually, but who's counting ;)

AUBREY 11:41 PM

Are you insane??? I can't drink that!!

MORGAN 11:42 PM

It's not like imma return it if you don't lmao

I rolled my eyes at the text and opened the bottle. Ellie jumped.

"Sorry baby, I should've warned you."

"It's okay," she said, too busy shoveling down cheese puffs to really care. I poured myself a glass and sent him another picture.

AUBREY 11:45 PM

Thank you then, Mr. Wallen ;)

MORGAN 11:47 PM

You're welcome Mrs. Wallen, how did you find my sign? ;)

AUBREY 11:48 PM

Slightly disturbing

MORGAN 11:49 PM

Claiming my territory, baby. And as soon as you get here and little Miss Ellie falls asleep, I'll show you that you're all mine now ;)

I felt my cheeks turning red and my heart started beating faster.

"Hey Andrew, any way we can go a little faster?"

Hello lovelies! So, I was thinking of writing a little smut in the next chapter. Do you guys like that? Or would you rather I stick with drama/romance type of stuff? Please don't be shy and feel free to give feedback, that's how I know what you guys like and how I can adapt the story to please my readers!

XO

LadyBug

Chapter 10

By the time we got to Sneedville, Ellie had already fallen asleep in the car. The insane amount of cheese puffs I had let her eat probably didn't help. Andrew pulled into the driveway of a big farmhouse. I looked out the window; no sign of Morgan. He got out of the car and came to open the door for me.

"Be careful, ma'am it's a little-" he started. I jumped out of the car, staring down at my now mud covered feet. "Muddy," he added, a few seconds too late. I giggled.

"You're fine, Andrew. It's nothing," I said in an attempt to appease the alarmed look on his face. I heard a dog bark and the porch light went on.

"Quiet, Boots," I heard a voice say sternly. Of course he's got a dog named Boots.

The minute he appeared on the porch, I remembered why I had come here. He looked as beautiful as ever, wearing a white, long sleeved shirt that really modeled just how defined his shoulders were. He smiled at me and my heart skipped a beat.

"Girl, do you fill them jeans nicely," he said, beaming at me. I giggled, unable to wipe the dumb grin off my face. He walked down the four little steps that led to the porch and stood in front of me, putting his hands on my waist and looking deep into my eyes. "Missed me?" he asked. I rolled my eyes and he laughed. "Where is Ellie?"

"She fell asleep in the car after having way too many snacks," I shrugged. He made a little visor with his hands and looked through the car window, checking on her.

"Aww, she looks so peaceful. Her bedroom's ready, I'll carry her in," he said, opening the door and unbuckling her seatbelt carefully. In that moment, I could see what a great dad he must have been. Josh had never done anything like that for Ellie. Whether it be getting a bedroom ready and comfortable for her, or carrying her little sleeping body out of the car without waking her up, Morgan had already, in the span of a few days, done more for Ellie than her dad had in her whole three years. I hadn't been sure about Morgan up until now and one of the main reasons for that was that I wanted to protect Ellie from yet another heartbreak. And yet, right now, his actions were showing me that he might be the best possible person to share mine and Ellie's life. I smiled at the thought before realizing Morgan was already on the porch, waiting for me to open the door.

"Sorry," I whispered, running to get the door.

"You're fine," he whispered, kissing the top of my head gently. I followed him down the hallway and into the bedroom. I couldn't believe what I saw next. He hadn't just 'made the room comfortable' for her. He had made it her bedroom. He had gotten the pictures of Ellie and I that I had posted on facebook framed and displayed them in the room. He had gotten these cute little wooden letters that spelled out ELLIE and put them up on the wall above the bed. The comforter was a light shade of pink and there was a star shaped night light on the nightstand. He put her down onto the bed gently, took off her shoes and put the blankets over her delicately. He put a finger over his mouth, telling me to be quiet and tip toed out of the room, closing the door silently.

"I can't believe you did all this," I said, deeply touched by the amount of effort he had put in to make this happen with very little time. He smiled.

"I wanted her to feel at home," he said nonchalantly, looking deep into my eyes. "I didn't know what she was into so I didn't get her any toys yet, but maybe tomorrow my mom could take you guys into the store and pick a few things for her? That way you'd get to meet her and see how she is with Ellie, and-"

"I'm sorry for ever doubting you," I cut him off, genuinely apologetic. "What you've done for Ellie tonight is truly remarkable. Thank you," I said, maintaining eye contact. He tilted his head slightly and I noticed the sweetest twinkle in his eyes. I'm really starting to fall for him.

"Anything to make you happy, baby," he whispered in my ear, his mouth slowly making its way down to my neck. I shivered and felt him grin against my skin. He wrapped his arms around me tightly, trailing kisses from my neck to my forehead, tickling me with his mustache along the way. I giggled and he tightened his grip around me, breathing in the smell of my hair.

"I missed you," he whispered.

"I missed you too," I admitted. He placed a kiss on top of my head highlighting our height difference, and let go of the embrace.

"Would you like to see our room, Mrs. Wallen?" he asked. I rolled my eyes.

"Don't I have to earn that title?" I raised an eyebrow.

"You're probably right, I guess you do, damn," he joked, intertwining our fingers and leading me further down the hallway. He opened the last door on the left and I followed him in. The room was nothing like what I'd imagined. I was expecting something that would almost resemble a college dorm or teenage boy's room. He didn't strike me as the type of man who would pay attention to the decor of his own bedroom. And yet, this room was beautifully designed. A black, king size canopy bed with dark gray bedding was the star of the show. The lighter gray, long haired decorative pillows matched the rug that was sticking out from either side of the bed. A beautiful black leather bench was resting by the foot of the bed, matching the oak sturdy vintage dressers and bedside tables. The smooth blades of mahogany adorn the antique black colored ceiling fan that was working full speed, but still didn't make a sound. A large flat screen TV was facing the bed on the opposite wall. And a couple of, what seemed to be very expensive, paintings were tastefully displayed across the room. I was baffled.

"You designed this yourself?" I asked, speechless. He scratched the back of his head.

"My kid's mom did a while back," he admitted. "I just never bothered changing it, I guess. But we can change it if you want, I'm not married to anything. This is your room just as much as it is mine now," he said, trying to make up for the initial answer. Great. Sleeping in another woman's bed. Just what I needed. "Different mattress, though," he added, tilting his head and giving me a faint little crooked smile. It was as though he had read my mind. I guess that does make things a little better. I wonder how many girls he's fucked in that bed. That last thought sent me spiraling. I sat down on the bench. Breathe in, breathe out, Aubrey.

"Baby?" he asked, pulling me out of my thoughts.

"Yeah?" I said, looking up to face him.

"I'm serious, we can change it if you don't like it," he said, softening his gaze.

"It's fine, I love it," I lied. The truth was that the design was beautifully executed. That woman had taste, there was no denying it. Both in bedroom sets AND in men. I just didn't know how comfortable I could possibly feel sleeping in a bedroom furnished by my new man's ex girlfriend.

"Really? 'Cause Imma be honest, you look kind of mortified right now," he said. "If that makes you feel any better you're the second woman to ever set foot in this room, and the first one to sleep on that mattress?" he stated. That did make me feel a little better.

"Really?"

"Yeah, do you think I bring random girls over to my parents' house?" he asked.

"So, you don't live here?" I asked.

"I have a house in Nashville, which can also be redecorated if that'll put your mind at ease," he joked. "But no, I don't live here. I just come here when I need to be with family. I grew up here, y'know." I nodded.

"Have you brought girls over to your other house?" I asked, afraid of what the answer would be.

"Honestly?" he asked. I nodded yes. "A couple. None of them as pretty as you, but I don't want to hide anything from you so yeah, it's happened. But that doesn't change anything about the way you make me feel, and that sure as hell doesn't mean I would do that now that I have you in my life," he assured me. I liked that he made room for my insecurities. Josh would've lost his patience with me already for asking all these questions. But Morgan didn't. Sure, he was hot, and famous, and probably very rich, but most of all he was kind, and patient and that impressed me a lot more than money and fame ever would.

"Thank you," I mumbled.

"Why?"

"Being honest, I guess," I answered, my eyes avoiding him.

"I want you to trust me. I know it'll be a process, I've met that asshole who bailed on you and Ellie and I get why you can be nervous about certain things, but I won't ever treat you the way he has. That much I can promise you. And no matter how long it takes until you feel comfortable enough to fully trust me, I'll stick around," he said, taking my hand into his. I didn't even know how to thank him. I felt horrible for judging his manners at first because no matter how rough that man looked, he was a true act of class. Then something he said popped back into my head.

"So, this is a new bed?" I asked.

"Yeah, I've only slept in it a couple times. By myself, I swear," he chuckled.

"So do you wanna-"

"Break it in?" he winked.

Granted, this is not the most exciting chapter I've published, but it has a bit pf character development and I promise the next one will make up for it! ;)

XO

LadyBug

Chapter 11 (smut)

✱ ****WARNING : MATURE/SEXUAL CONTENT*** AS PER USUAL IF YOU DON'T LIKE SMUT YOU CAN SKIP THE CHAPTER ENTIRELY AND THE STORY WILL STILL MAKE SENSE**

We had been making out on the bench for a solid ten minutes, yet all our clothes were still on. I could feel through his jeans just how hard he was, unwillingly rubbing his erection onto my thigh. I knew he didn't want to pressure me into anything, especially with everything that had gone on between us over the last couple of days. But I wanted to be with him that way, and him being respectful right now was not what I needed. C'mon, Aubrey. He doesn't want you to be shy. Be a big girl and touch him already. I moved my right hand slowly from the back of his neck, onto the bulge in his jeans and rubbed it lightly. He groaned into my mouth.

"I want you so fucking bad right now, baby" he whispered in my ear.

"Yeah?" I whispered back, undoing the button of his jeans and letting my hand roam free inside his boxers. I wrapped my fingers softly around his cock and took it out of his pants, stroking it slowly. He bit his bottom lip and exhaled slowly, staring at my hand on his dick.

"Mmm," he moaned softly, closing his eyes and letting his head fall back. I got down on my knees with his cock still in my hand and checked that his eyes were still closed before slowly sliding the tip of my tongue up the underside of his dick, feeling it twitch. He opened his eyes and looked at me.

"Holy shit, you're hot," he panted, twisting my hair up in his fingers. I licked my lips softly before sliding them around the tip of his cock, swirling my tongue around it. He pulled on my hair slightly, forcing me to look into his lustful, half-lidded eyes. I let my lips follow my hand further down his shaft, and further still until my hand hit the base, not breaking eye contact. He twitched, bucking his hips into my mouth.

"Sorry, I- Ughh", he mumbled. Look who's in charge now, player. I felt the head of his cock pressing against the back of my throat and wrapped my lips tightly around the base, tasting the salty pre-cum drip on the back of my tongue. I pushed my head forward a couple of times, grinding his cock into my throat, feeling it spasm. He pushed his hips into my face, pressing even more tightly into my throat. I gagged. Fuck.

"Shit, I'm sorry," he mumbled, grazing my cheek with his thumb and winking at me. Holy shit he's so hot. I can't believe he's mine. I pushed my head back onto his cock, and his sounds of pleasure, combined with the fact that he was literally the hottest man on earth, made me start to squirm. I could feel my clit pulsing against my silk underwear and selfishly sneaked a hand into my jeans, rubbing it slowly, with his dick still in my mouth. His eyes were closed and his head had rolled back, facing the ceiling. As I teased myself, I worked harder on him, letting my tongue glide over his skin as I stroked my clit. Suddenly he pushed me off him, gently enough not to hurt me, but firmly enough to let me know that my time of taking charge was over. He stood up, taking my hand out of my underwear and fully undressing before my eyes. I stayed quiet, staring him down, still not completely over how good he looked.

"Lay down on the bed," he ordered. I bit my lip and did as told, still fully dressed. He unzipped my pants and took them off me, leaving my underwear on.

"Take off your shirt," he said sternly, watching me execute myself. "Good girl," he praised once I was done, letting his hands run over my naked breasts.

"Now let me make something clear," he whispered into my ear, laying over me, moving my panties to the side and giving his fingers access to my pussy. "I take care care of you," he said, sliding a finger inside me. I let out a needy moan, instantly trying to cover my mouth. He chuckled.

"That's right," he whispered, adding another finger and kissing my neck softly.

"Oh my god, baby," I squirmed. He smiled against my neck and pulled his fingers out of me. He held my panties to the side with his thumb and threw my legs over his shoulders roughly, aligning himself perfectly and slowly pushing his cock inside of me. I whimpered and gripped the side of the bed with my fingertips.

"Fuck, I missed you," he groaned, slowly fucking into me, his fingers digging into my thighs. I looked into his half-closed eyes and could feel the burn of his gaze on my body. In that moment, I truly felt, for the first time, like he was mine and I was his. He pinned my hips firmly against the mattress so I would stop squirming and started thrusting faster, making my body crave his more with each pump. I love you.

"I missed you too," I panted, barely audible. He locked his lips with mine, pressing my legs against my chest and thrusting deeper inside of me. I moaned as he kept hitting the right spot.

"Baby, I'm gonna cum," he groaned.

"Don't cum inside me," I said, shoving him slightly, forcing him to pull out, which he did just in time to cum on my stomach like a Pollock painting. He let himself fall down onto the bed next to me catching his breath while I grabbed a few tissues to clean myself up.

"Why not inside? What's up with that?"

Jackson Pollock is definitely gonna come haunt me for that line lmao

XO

LadyBug

Chapter 12

There was a couple of seconds of silence before he spoke again.

"But you are on the pill, right?" he asked, turning towards me. I didn't answer. "Aubrey?" he tried again.

"I hadn't had sex in three years, I couldn't have known it would happen," I mumbled.

"Three years?!" he yelled.

"Shhh," I shushed him.

"Three years, Aubrey?," he whispered. I rolled my eyes and looked away.

"Alright, good talk," I said, pushing him further away from me onto the bed.

"Baby, don't take it like that," he said softly, wrapping his arms around me and pulling me back in. "I just mean, like, why? You're a very pretty girl, I just don't understand," he whispered.

"I don't know, the occasion just didn't present itself," said. He chuckled.

"Girl, you know Jared would have loved to fix that for ya, right?"

"Well, I'm not like you!" I snapped.

"What's that supposed to mean?"

"I can't just sleep with anyone; I'm not one of those girls," I said. He rolled his eyes.

"The girls I've been with don't necessarily sleep with just anyone," he defended himself.

"That's really the hill you wanna die on?" I inquired, raising an eyebrow.

"Look, picture this: you're at a bar in Burlington and young Johnny Depp shows up. Even if you don't usually sleep with random men, you're telling me you wouldn't try and get a piece of that?"

"Are you comparing yourself to young Johnny Depp, right now?" I asked, audibly judging him by the tone of my voice.

"No I- You know what, nevermind," he laughed. "But I'm making you an appointment tomorrow to get that pill cause ain't no way I'm gonna glaze you up like a toaster strudel every time we have sex."

"Morgan! That's so crass!" I said, feeling my cheeks turn red. He laughed and kissed the top of my head.

"Tired?" he asked. I nodded. "Alright, let's get to bed," he said, turning off the lights and getting into bed. I got under the blankets and he pulled me into his arms. "I'm really glad you're here," he whispered, placing a gentle kiss on my forehead. I smiled to myself and slowly, I dozed off into his arms.

***

I woke up the next morning to the smell of freshly cooked bacon. I quickly checked my phone; 11:00 AM. I jumped out of bed and immediately got dressed, quickly throwing on sweatpants and a t-shirt and putting my hair up into a ponytail.

"Ellie?" I called, making my way down the hallway.

"In here, mama!" She yelled from the living room. I followed her voice and found her sitting on the floor playing with her barbie dolls with a woman I assumed was Morgan's mom.

"Hi, I hope you don't mind, we decided to let you sleep in a little," the woman said, smiling at me. She had long dirty-blonde hair, amazing cheekbones and gorgeous blue eyes, just like his. "I'm Lesli, by the way. Morgan's mom," she smiled.

"I'm Aubrey," I said. "Ellie's mom," I added jokingly. She laughed.

"Isn't she the sweetest little girl," she said, pinching Ellie's little toes and making her laugh. I smiled. Ellie looked so at ease already. She really was good with kids. I looked around the room, trying to figure out where Morgan was.

"He's in the shower," Lesli said, noticing my eyes scanning the room. "Should be out any minute now, but please, grab some coffee and make yourself at home. It's been a while since he's had a woman in his life that he felt he could bring home to his mama. I'm very excited that we get to have you with us," she winked. I smiled.

"That's very nice of you to say," I smiled timidly.

"Morgan told me that you might be a little shy at first, but I think we'll get along great. And hopefully, by the end of the week you can get a good sense of who I am and feel comfortable enough to trust me with little miss Ellie," she said, tickling Ellie who couldn't stop laughing. I giggled at the scene.

"Aren't you a sight for sore eyes," I heard a voice say behind me. I couldn't help but to smile. I turned around to face him and he immediately placed a gentle peck on my lips. I breathed in his fresh shower smell while his wet hair dripped all over the floor.

"You smell good," I said softly. He leaned in for another kiss, but our lips didn't get to touch before Lesli interrupted him.

"Boy, you're dripping all over my floor. Go dry that hair before I have to mop the entire house," she scolded him.

"Sorry, mama," he chuckled, squeezing my butt slightly and winking at me before making his way back into the bathroom.

"I swear, that kid will be the death of me," she laughed.

"That bad, huh?" I asked.

"One day it'll be your house that he messes up. You tell me then," she laughed. I smiled at the thought. The idea of having a house with him, a house that would have no history but the one we made together, was giving me butterflies. I had no idea what he had been telling his mom about me, but the way she was treating me was leading me to believe that he must have had genuine feelings for me. She seemed confident that we would be a part of each other's life for a good amount of time and had gone out of her way to make Ellie and I feel at home. I could already tell how kind that woman was and it really helped put my mind at ease. Seeing where Morgan came from was actually helping me overcome some of the fears I had been having. Getting to talk to his mom and seeing how authentic she was gave me a good idea of the way she must've raised her son.

"I was thinking of taking Ellie to get some new toys for her room this afternoon. I doubt Morgan will want to come, he tends to avoid public appearances when he can, but maybe we could make this a girls trip?" she said invitingly.

"Sure," I smiled. "I know Ellie would love that."

"And so would I, Aubrey."

***

We got to the store and walked through the aisles with Ellie in tow, touching every toy within her reach.

"So, Morgan tells me you're from Vermont? How do you like it there?" Lesli asked, making casual conversation.

"I like Vermont, I'm originally from Portland, Maine though. I moved to Vermont to be with my dad when he got sick," I confessed.

"Aren't you a doll? Hopefully, he's all better now."

"He passed away before Ellie was born, actually. Liver cancer."

"Oh, I'm sorry, honey. I didn't mean to... God rest his soul," she said empathetically.

"Thank you," I smiled faintly.

"How about your mom? Does she still live in Maine?"

"I'm not sure actually. She calls once in a blue moon, asking for money, but that's about it. I was 18 the last time I saw her, she's never even seen Ellie. Nor has she expressed any interest to," I admitted. "Ellie's the only family I have, really."

"Well, not anymore, darling. You have us now," she said, wrapping her right arm around my shoulders and squeezing them gently. "It was about time I saw my son with a nice girl by his side. I've had a hard time accepting some of his past... choices. You always want what's best for your kids and you have no idea how many nights I prayed that someone like you would come into his life. A good woman with a good heart who would encourage him to make the right choices," she said. "I'm really glad you decided to give him a chance after all. He would kill me if he knew I told you this but you have no idea how disappointed he was when you decided not to come. He had called me on the phone the night before telling me how he was bringing home the girl of his dreams and how I would be so happy to get a bonus grandchild, he was so excited. When I saw him getting out of that truck by himself, all disappointed, my heart broke," she said. From mom to mom, I knew what she meant. Seeing your kids hurting is worse than being hurt yourself.

"I didn't mean to hurt him, I just had to be sure, you know," I explained. "Jared had said some things and I needed to make sure he was serious before dragging Ellie into this."

"Oh, honey. You do not have to justify a single thing to me. I know my son, I know he's not perfect and he comes with his set of challenges. And I know Jared, he's a fine young man and I'm sure he had his reasons to tell you what he told you, but Aubrey, as God is my witness, if my son doesn't treat you right, you come to me, honey. I'll give him a piece of my mind. You sweet, sweet girl," she said, gently squeezing my arm. The more time I spent with this woman, the more she felt like the mom I had always wished to have. Morgan didn't know how lucky he was to come home to a woman like this everyday growing up. Someone so kind and supportive.

"Thank you Mrs. Wallen," I said.

"Oh please, if you don't want to call me mom, at the very least call me Lesli."

So, I know these last few chapters have not been the most exciting but I have things coming up to make up for it! I know this hasn't been getting as many votes in the last couple of days so I hope you guys are still engaging with my content! If there are things you don't like/want less of or things you absolutely love/want more of, please let me know!! I absolutely love getting your feedback!

XO

Chapter 13

We headed back home with a trunk full of brand new toys for Ellie who had fallen asleep in the backseat.

"You didn't have to spoil her that much, Lesli," I stated, almost embarrassed by the small fortune she had just spent on my daughter.

"Oh, nonsense. If God didn't want that child to be a little spoiled, He would have known better than to put her on my path," she joked. She pulled into the driveway and I immediately sensed something was wrong. Morgan was standing on the porch, his cell phone glued to his ear, seemingly having a very heated discussion. I could tell just by his body language that he was angry. He kept pacing back and forth, moving his arms as he spoke, his hands curled up into fists.

"Uh-oh," Lesli said. "That can't be good."

I felt my blood run cold in my veins. As soon as the car had stopped moving, I swung the door open and jumped out.

"Morgan!" I yelled, hoping he would give me some type of hint as to what was going on. He looked at me and lifted his index finger, gesturing to me to wait. I walked towards him and sat on one of the two rocking chairs that were displayed on the porch, trying to make out as much as I could from a one sided conversation.

"What the fuck do you mean you didn't see what happened?! Who the fuck leaves a two year old kid play with a 100 pound dog by himself?! Are you out of your fucking mind?!"

Was that about his son? Had something happened to his kid? My heart sank into my chest. I couldn't imagine what I would be going through if something happened to Ellie.

"Morgan, what is going on?" his mom yelled from the car, waking up Ellie who started crying. I got up from my chair and went to get my daughter, unable to hear what he was saying from across the driveway.

"It's okay, baby," I told Ellie. "Mama's here," I said, getting her out of her car seat and into my arms. She nuzzled my neck as I held her tight, turning towards Morgan to see if he was still on the phone. He wasn't. He was holding on to the railing of the porch, looking as though he had just seen a ghost. His skin looked several shades paler than it usually did and I could tell from the look in his eyes that there was something seriously wrong. I put Ellie down and walked towards him.

"We have to go," he said, walking hastily towards me.

"Where?" I asked.

"Nashville," he said, grabbing my hand and pulling me towards his Chevy truck. "Ellie, will you be a good girl for me and stay with Grandma Lesli?" he asked softly, kneeling down to her level. She smiled, swiftly looked at his mom and nodded yes. He smiled at her. "Alright, I promise you that your mama will call you as soon as she can and that we will be back in no time, alright pumpkin?" he asked. She nodded again.

"Will someone tell me what is going on?" Lesli asked.

"Katie called, her fucking dog attacked Indie," he said, his voice trembling. "Bit him in the face, he's in the hospital. Get in the truck, Aubrey," he said impatiently. His mom pulled him to the side, trying to calm him down while I hugged Ellie goodbye and promised her I would facetime her as soon as I got to Nashville. I got in the truck and Morgan slammed the door, quickly driving away.

Most of the drive was spent quietly, with Morgan speeding and frequently switching lanes to pass slower cars. He braked abruptly, almost crashing into the car in front of us, aggressively honking at it.

"Maybe you should slow down a little," I mumbled nervously.

"Would you ask me to slow down if it was Ellie?" he snapped. I didn't respond, but I knew he was right; I don't think I would. He went around the car and went back to speeding down the highway. An hour after that, we were in the hospital walking towards his son's room.

"Should I come in with you? I don't want to offend her," I said, panting as he dragged me down the corridors.

"Offend who?"

"His mom?" I said. He chuckled dryly.

"See if I care."

"Morgan, I-"

"I want you with me. I need you right now, Aubrey. Can you please do this for me?" he said, slowing down to look into my eyes. I could see the despair in his gaze and I didn't want to let him down. I would probably want to have someone by my side as well if I was going through something like that. I nodded. "Thank you," he said, kissing my forehead softly.

"Seriously, Mo? Seriously?" A voice emerged from the room to our left, and a skinny, blonde woman came out. She calls him Mo... They have history. Of course they do, they have a freaking child together, what did you think, Aubrey?! I shouldn't be here.

"Can't even come see your son in the hospital without having a groupie tagging along?!" she snapped. I felt so out of place, I wanted to melt into the floor.

"I'm not doing this with you right now, Katie," he said, walking in the room, dragging me by the hand. She put her arm in front of him, denying him access. "What the fuck?!"

"She's not coming in," she said, staring me down with disdain.

"Are you out of your goddamn mind-"

"It's fine. Go be with your son, I'll wait outside," I said, not wanting to cause a scene. He looked at me, trying to figure out whether this was some sort of trap. I nodded softly, giving him a faint smile and squeezing his hand gently. "Go, I'll be fine," I assured him. He kissed me gently and I could feel the gaze of his son's mom burning a hole in the side of my head. He pulled away and slowly let go of my hand, walking in the room followed by the girl. She was gorgeous. Her body was so effortlessly skinny and her sunflower blond hair flowed perfectly down her slightly arched back. You could tell that she'd had some work done, but most of it was tasteful. Even taking her son to the hospital, she still managed to look put together. She wasn't just pretty, she was Hollywood pretty. And definitely a lot prettier than me. I wanted to hate her, I wanted to be mad over the way she had treated me, but the truth was that I understood. If Josh had showed up to the hospital for Ellie with a woman I had never seen before in my life, I can't tell you with certainty that I would have reacted differently. She had every right to be upset and I didn't want to judge her based on that encounter alone.

Morgan had been in the room for a solid hour and I was still sitting on the same bench, waiting for him a few doors down the corridor. I pulled out my phone and called Lesli, hoping to talk to Ellie. It rang twice and she picked up.

"Hello?"

"Hi, it's Aubrey, I was hop-"

"Any news?" she interrupted me.

"Not really, uh, Morgan's with him right now, but I haven't seen him."

"Why? Hospital policy?" she asked.

"Something like that," I lied.

"Aubrey?"

"Yes?"

"I can tell when someone's hiding something from me. What's going on?" she asked. I sighed.

"It's just, his ex didn't want me in the room, which I totally understand, so unfortunately I don't have news for you. I wish I did but-"

"That woman is vile," she spat, putting an end to my rumbling. "Always up in his business, trying to do as much damage as she can. Do me a favor, sweetheart?"

"Uh, sure?"

"Do not let that girl get to you. Nothing that comes out of that mouth is worth listening to. You're a good woman and my son is crazy about you. Do not let her mess with your head," she warned.

"O-okay," I mumbled, not quite sure of what to do with these instructions. "Can I speak to Ellie?" I asked.

"Of course," she said. "Ellie, your mama's on the phone," she said.

"Hi, mama," I heard her little voice say as she took the phone.

"Hi, baby, is everything going well?"

"Yes, grandma Lesli is helping me put away my new toys in my room," she giggled, excited.

"That's so fun, baby!"

"Will you be back before I go to bed, mama?"

"I don't think so, Ellie. Not tonight, but I will send you a magical kiss so that you sleep peacefully through the night and mama will be back in no time, okay?"

"Okay. I love you," she mumbled.

"I love you too, baby."

"Aubrey!" I heard Morgan call from outside of his son's room. I waved for him to see me and finished up the call quickly.

"You have a good night now, pumpkin!"

"Thanks, mama. Byyyye," she said before hanging up. I got up and walked towards Morgan.

"Is he okay?" I asked.

"Yeah, he'll be fine," he said, scratching the back of his head. "He will need stitches though."

"Oh my god, poor thing."

"We're gonna sleep in Nashville tonight and take him home to my mom's tomorrow as soon as he can leave," he explained.

"You're not taking him to Knoxville, he's coming home with me," a voice said. His son's mom poked her head out of the door.

"You think you're taking him home to the dog who attacked him? Girl, you must be out of your damn mind. I swear to god he will not set foot in that house until that dog is gone."

"You're not taking my son to go play house with your little girlfriend. How old is she anyway?"

"Older than that boytoy of yours, whom I might mention has been inside the room this entire time. You have made it very clear in the past that we get to introduce our son to whomever we feel comfortable introducing him to, and even when I didn't agree with your choices, I bit my tongue and stayed respectful. So you're gonna have to learn to do the same thing-"

"Respectful?! Was cheating on me respectful, Mo?" she snapped. I started feeling more and more uncomfortable with every passing second.

"I can leave you two if you need to talk things over, it's-"

"No," Morgan said. "No, she will not bully you into leaving, again," he added before turning back to her. "I'm not doing this with you. I'm not here for you, I'm here for my son. You can believe whatever you want, but I'm not gonna fight with you. I'm bringing Indie home tomorrow, it'll give you time to re-home the dog and then you can come get him. Please, don't complicate things," he said calmly. I was genuinely shocked at how calm he was in this situation. She was getting more and more heated, which I understood; situations like these are emotional, but he got his point across while remaining calm and in control. I admired that.

"Take it as an opportunity to find a good home for your dog, yeah?" he asked softly, putting his hand on her shoulder. It was hard not to let jealousy get in the way. I knew he had loved her, and I saw the way he looked at her. It was like they could communicate without even speaking. He knew her eyes better than he knew mine and I'd be lying if I said that didn't sting a little. But part of me was genuinely happy for him. He got to co-parent with someone who was involved and genuinely cared about his kid. That was more than I could say for myself.

"Yeah, okay," she finally sighed. She turned towards me "I'm sorry, I'm sure you're a nice gir-"

"It's fine, don't even worry about it," I assured her, smiling faintly.

"Imma go kiss him goodbye and then we'll leave?" Morgan asked, taking my hand into his softly. I nodded and he kissed my forehead.

"Okay, be right back," he said, walking back in the room.

This one is slightly longer than my usual chapter, I hope you guys like it!

XO

Chapter 14

"I can't stand that girl," he said, driving through the streets of Nashville.

"It's fine, I mean, she apologized," I tried to reassure him.

"She's not sorry, she's manipulating you! See how she purposely dropped that I had cheated on her, right in front of you?! Everything she does is calculated. She's so fucking petty," he said, obviously agitated.

"Well did you?" I asked, not sure I was ready to hear his answer.

"Did I what?"

"Cheat on her?"

"No!" he said, visibly annoyed I had even asked.

"Okay, sorry I asked I just-"

"I have never cheated on that girl. The whole time we were together, I was nothing but a gentleman to her. I fucking asked her to marry me and yet she'd rather believe some dumb rumors and spread lies about me than to give me the benefit of the doubt. Someone said I had cheated on her, a fucking throwaway account on instagram, and she ran with it." They were engaged.

"Why would you even cheat on her, she's so pretty," I mumbled, feeling so incredibly small.

"She used to be, until she messed up her whole face," he spat.

"What do you mean?"

"You think I like that shit? The whole plastic look? She didn't look like that when I was with her," he said, which, I hated to admit, made me feel a little bit better about my untouched, makeup-free face. "She made a fool out of me," he continued. "Broke up with me and broke my heart, dragging my name in the mud for the whole world to see, telling people how I was toxic and unfaithful, spewing all kinds of lies just for the fun of it."

"Maybe she felt betrayed," I said softly.

"Betrayed?! How do you think I felt?! Exposing our business in front of the whole world and then trying to mend things and get back together, what the fuck did she think would happen," he snapped. "Trapping me into having a kid with her."

"Woah, Morgan. Don't say shit like that, you can't take back that kind of stuff."

"Look, I love my son. God gave me my son for a reason and I am incredibly grateful, I wouldn't trade him for the world. But the way she made it happen is shady as fuck and she definitely did it on purpose. We had been broken up for some months and she came to a show, waited until I was black out drunk to get me into bed and called me not even two weeks later telling me she was pregnant and telling me her doctor was 'so impressed she knew so soon'. You think she didn't have that shit planned? You know, the amount of child support that I pay for Indie could support 10 of them kids! How do you think she got all that botox? That girl has been living on my dime since the day she got pregnant and she'll be mooching off me 'til the day I die," he said, obviously heated.

"I'm not defending her, but it is hard being a single parent. Why would anyone choose to do that?"

"You're not defending her but it sounds a hell of a lot like you are," he spat. "And it is hard for single moms like you, Aubrey, I know that, but don't compare the two of you. She has nannies and staff and gets an insane amount of money from me monthly and I still take my son whenever I can. My mom takes him too when I'm touring and working and when I'm not, I have him with me half the time. She doesn't work, she doesn't have to worry about financial stuff and I take my responsibilities very seriously. It has nothing to do with your situation."

"I'm sorry, I didn't mean to offend you," I mumbled. He put his hand on my thigh gently and sighed.

"You're fine, I'm sorry I dumped all of that on you," he breathed, calming himself down.

"You're fine."

"I just hate the way she treated you," he admitted.

"It's alright, Morgan, really. I've been through worse," I assured him. He pulled into the driveway of a beautiful two story house and opened the garage door with this little remote from inside the car.

"That's your house?" I asked, baffled by how big and modern the space looked.

"Yeah, I'm probably gonna sell it soon. It's too public now, and this asshole neighbor keeps filming me whenever he gets a chance," he said, pointing to the house across from his. I opened the door and hopped out of the car, genuinely exhausted.

"After you," he said, opening the door that led to the inside of the house. I walked in and looked around. The dark hardwood floors matched the railing of the stairs perfectly. The walls were painted all white, offering a nice contrast to the dark, modern furniture and the light marble countertops glowed in the soft wattage lighting. Just like in his bedroom, the design had been tastefully executed.

"Who designed this one?" I asked. "Katie again?" He chuckled.

"Fuck no, I had someone come in and decorate it for me."

"It does look slightly more like a bachelor pad than your bedroom does," I admitted.

"That's because it is," he said. I furrowed my brows. 'Or was, before this beautiful lady came into my life," he saved, pulling me in for a kiss. "Hungry?" he asked.

"Starving," I admitted.

"I haven't been here in weeks, I doubt I have much, but we can order in if you want," he said walking towards the kitchen. He opened the fridge and checked inside to see if he had anything that could be whipped up quickly when I noticed a piece of red, lacy fabric on the counter top. I lifted it to see what it was and immediately threw it back where I first found it. Panties. The back of my neck suddenly felt burning hot and nausea overcame me. I inhaled slowly and exhaled, closing my eyes. I could hear Morgan rumbling through the fridge.

"What the fuck," I said, trying to contain myself.

"What?" he said, turning back to face me. "What's up?"

I pointed to the red underwear that was crumpled on the counter and he looked at it, mortified. He grabbed it quickly and threw it in the trash, not saying a single word.

"Whose is it?" I asked.

"I don't know," he said.

"Cut the crap."

"I swear I don't know! Some girl, a friend of a friend of Ernest's wife. I don't know her name," he rambled, clearly panicking.

"You don't know her name..?"

"I mean, I'm sure she told me, I just I don't rememb-"

"That is so much worse," I said, honestly disgusted.

"I haven't been here in weeks, Aubrey. What do you want me to say, that was before I knew you. Things have changed now," he said, trying to take my hands into his. I pulled away quickly.

"Don't touch me," I snapped.

"Please don't make a big deal out of this-"

"You don't know her name, Morgan?! Really?! That means there's been a lot of them. How many? What's your number, huh? What am I? Dumb bitch #10,000?!"

"No! I don't know, why does it matter?! We didn't even know each other!"

"Well, maybe you should have had someone come clean your mess before bringing yet another girl home, don't you think?! Don't I at least deserve that?! To be the 10000th girl you've fucked is one thing, but for you to make me feel like just another number, that's a whole other thing."

"Aubrey, I would have, but it's not like we exactly planned to come here! I'm sorry that I didn't think of having a maid come over when I was speeding to get to the hospital to see my son! I'm sorry this isn't up to your standards!" he snapped. I felt tears well up in my eyes.

"Can I go take a shower or am I gonna find someone else's thong in there too," I said, my voice trembling. He sighed, and took a step towards me.

"Aubrey, I-"

"I just want a shower, Morgan," I whispered, a single tear rolling down my cheek.

"The bathroom's clean," he whispered, wiping my cheek with his thumb. "I'm sorry," he added.

"Thank you," I whispered, my voice cracking. I ignored his apology and made my way to the bathroom, my heart heavy and my brain spiraling.

I'm fully aware it's kind of a waste of content to update twice in less than two hours but my brain couldn't leave the story at chapter 13 'cause it's "not a good number", so hopefully you guys enjoy lmao!

Chapter 15

I let the hot water burn my skin as if that would erase the dirty feeling that inhabited my body. I knew he hadn't done it on purpose. I knew his intention had never been to hurt me or make me feel like one among many other women. And most importantly, I knew his heart was in the right place. But I still couldn't shake the feeling that maybe I wasn't cut out for this. Maybe dating someone so famous, someone with a reputation for being a womanizer, wasn't right for me. Maybe I was too insecure, too sensitive to be able to cope with the constant impression of being compared to the -probably- hundreds of women who had set foot here before me and of not measuring up. I looked down at my body, my eyes staring at the scar the c-section had left when I had given birth to Ellie. I was willing to bet good money that little miss red-lace-panties didn't have a single scar or roll of fat on her. This isn't healthy. I heard a knock on the bathroom door.

"What?" I asked.

"Can I come in?" I heard Morgan ask softly.

"No, I'm not dressed," I said, turning the water off and getting out of the shower. "Where are the towels?" I asked as the water dripped off my body and turned into a puddle all over the ceramic floor.

"In the cabinet on the left," he said calmly. I frantically searched through said cabinet without finding a single towel.

"They're not there," I said impatiently.

"They're supposed to be," Morgan said. "Can I please come in? I'll give you a towel and we can talk."

"No, I'm not dressed!" I repeated.

"I think we're past that point, Aubrey. Just let me get you a damn towel," he said, opening the door. I quickly sat on the floor, bringing my knees up to my chest and covering myself up the best I could, feeling my eyes well up with tears. He opened the cabinet on the right and unfolded a towel. He got on his knees to be at my level and placed the towel gently on my shoulders, squeezing them softly to rub the water off.

"You said the cabinet on the left," I mumbled.

"My left, your right. I'm sorry," he whispered. I looked down and he lifted my chin with two of his fingers, forcing me to look into his eyes. "What's going on?"

"I have scars."

"I mean, don't we all?"

"I mean physically, like on my body, from my c-section and-"

"And?"

"And rolls on my back."

"Okay? So?"

"And I don't wear red lacy underwear."

"Aubrey-"

"I'm not Hollywood pretty like your son's mom and-"

"Hollywood pretty?"

"You know, like the Kardashians and stuff," I mumbled. He chuckled and took my hands into his.

"I don't want you to be 'Hollywood pretty' and I sure as hell don't want you to look like my ex," he said softly. "How about when you start spiraling about other women I've been with, you take a second to realize that out of all these people, you're the one I chose to bring home to my mom?" he suggested. I smiled faintly. He was right. I had been so absorbed by my insecurities that I hadn't even tried seeing things from his perspective. Even his mom had said that he hadn't brought a girl home in a really long time. He had spent the last couple of years of his life being on the road and meeting women who wanted nothing more than to wake up next to him in the morning. He had options; a lot of options. And out of all these options he had picked me. He had made sacrifices for me. I had been so wrapped up in the idea that our relationship would ruin my friendship with Jared that I had failed to recognize that he had put his friendship with him in jeopardy too. He was one of his oldest friends and yet, unlike me, he never, not for a second, thought of putting that friendship ahead of our relationship. I had to find a way to stop focusing on the flaws and actually take the time to realize that the man who was sitting on the floor in front of me had done nothing but prove to me that he would choose me, every chance he got.

"You're right. It's not fair of me to constantly bring up your past. I have to stop letting my insecurities get in the way of things," I admitted.

"And please, stop comparing yourself to other women. The minute I laid eyes on you at that baseball game, I knew right away you'd change my life. You're beautiful, Aubrey. Way more than you think. And the scar on your stomach?" he said, moving the towel and grazing it softly with his thumb. "You got it by bringing an amazing little girl into this world. You should be proud of that scar."

"I'm sorry that I'm such a mess," I said, slowly getting off the floor. He chuckled.

"See, I knew you were gonna be trouble," he laughed. I rolled my eyes. "I love you," he said.

"You do..?" I asked, almost unsure that I had heard that correctly.

"Were you ever doubting that?" he asked.

"No, it's just- You've never told me before," I said timidly. He placed the wet strand of hair that was in my face behind my ear delicately and grazed my cheek softly with his thumb, looking deep into my eyes.

"If you let me, I will tell you every single day for the rest of my life," he whispered, placing a warm kiss on my forehead.

"I love you too," I whispered back.

Okay, so, this is super short, and it's probably the most disgustingly lovey dovey thing I've ever written, but I'm a sucker for cheesy romance so I kind of just had fun with it! Hope you guys like it!

XO

LadyBug

Chapter 16

I opened my eyes and noticed the bed was empty. I slowly stretched my arms and looked at the time: 9:07 AM. I think I've slept in more often this week than I have in the last three years. I heard singing coming from the kitchen and got out of bed immediately. I threw on a pair of panties and one of Morgan's t-shirts and walked down the stairs, following the voice. I had never heard him sing before, but I could see now why his songs were #1. His voice was so raspy and beautiful, full of this ineffable southern charm everyone raved about. He had earphones in and was singing 'Give Me One Reason by Tracy Chapman' while pouring pancake batter into a hot pan. I giggled at the scene but he couldn't hear me. I walked up to him and poked him in the side. He jumped.

"Girl, don't creep up on me like that! I damn near knocked you out," he chuckled, taking his earbuds out and pulling me in for a hug. "Good morning, sleeping beauty," he said, kissing my lips gently.

"Your voice is beautiful," I smiled.

"It pays the bills," he shrugged humbly. "How did you sleep?"

"Like a baby," I said, stretching my back. "Smells good, I didn't know you cooked."

"I can cook pancakes and boil pasta," he laughed. "But, Indie says I make the 'best pancakes in the whole world', so, I guess I've perfected one recipe."

"Well, well, well, quite the chef you are," I joked.

"Oh and I called Jared this morning, he's gonna email you a prescription for the pill," he said nonchalantly.

"You what?!"

"I mean, he is a doctor," he shrugged.

"Morgan! I don't need Jared to be a part of my sex life!"

"Well, apparently you don't need anyone to be a part of your sex life, jeez. 3 years, woman?! What are you, a damn monk?" he teased.

"You're a dick," I laughed, shoving him playfully.

"Your virginity, the sequel," he continued.

"Stop!" I laughed. "You're just mad 'cause you're a whore and I'm not," I teased. He opened his mouth and put a hand to his chest, acting offended. I giggled.

"Alright, eat up! We have to go get Indie from the hospital in an hour," he said, sliding a plate of pancakes in front of me and drenching it in maple syrup.

"Woah there, that's enough syrup."

"Indie says it's part of the recipe," he winked.

"Yeah, well I'm not a 2 year old, I don't need a sugar rush," I giggled.

***

We got to the hospital and Katie was already waiting for us outside the room.

"Hey," she smiled. I smiled back.

"Hey," Morgan said dryly. "Why are you outside the room?"

"I was actually hoping I could talk to you," she said looking at me. Morgan raised an eyebrow.

"What could you possibly have to say to her?"

"Privately," she added, ignoring Morgan's question.

"Are you serious right now?" he asked, obviously getting more agitated.

"Daddy!" his son called from inside the room.

"Hi, monkey," he said, waving at him.

"Come sit with me!" Indie requested. Morgan gave Katie a warning look and walked into the room, sitting on the foot of the hospital bed. She pulled me to the side so we'd be out of earshot and I started picking at my fingernails nervously.

"I know we haven't had the best start, but I wanted to formally introduce myself. Hopefully we can get along. I'm Katie, by the way," she said, shaking my hand.

"Sure, um, Aubrey," I introduced myself. "And, like I told Morgan, I don't hold it against you. I would've probably acted the same way if it had been my daughter in that bed," I assured her.

"Oh, you're a mom?"

"Yeah, I have a three year old daughter, Ellie."

"Oh, wow. How old were you when you had her?" she asked. I could already feel the judgment in her tone.

"19."

"Wow, that's young. Well, look, I'm not trying to spoil your fun or anything, but," Here we go. "I'd hold off on introducing my kid to Morgan if I were you. I know him and he always does this thing where he gets super involved with these women and the second he leaves to go on tour, he messes things up, if you know what I mean," she said, sucking her teeth. "I know he's leaving this week so, maybe wait until he gets back, see if it lasts," she suggested, scrunching her nose.

"I'm actually going with him," I stated.

"On tour?" she asked. I nodded. "You're bringing your daughter?"

"Oh, no. Lesli will watch her and we'll fly her in every now and then."

"Oh, so you've met Lesli?"

"Yeah, such a sweet woman," I commented. She raised her eyebrows at my comment and gave me one of the fakest smiles I'd ever seen.

"I guess we're just different types of moms, I don't think I could ever leave Indie for that long," she said, obviously irritated to know Morgan had asked me to come with him. I tried to bite my tongue, I really did but I couldn't.

"Yeah, I guess we really are different types of moms 'cause see, I would never let my kid play with a large dog unsupervised," I smiled. She didn't say anything back, probably too shocked to even speak. And I'd be lying if I said I wasn't shocked at my own behavior. It wasn't like me to take a dig at someone, especially someone I didn't know well. But this girl was something else. I didn't know if it stemmed from jealousy or if she just genuinely had something against me, but I sure as hell wasn't about to let her stick her nose into my relationship. Especially after both Morgan and Lesli had warned me not to.

"Excuse me," I said, walking past her and making my way into the room. "Ready to go?" I asked Morgan.

"Yep, Indie, say bye to mama," he said softly, grabbing the diaper bag and putting the little boy on his hip. Indie waved his mom goodbye and blew her a few kisses, and we made our way to the parking lot. He was the absolute cutest, little blond kid ever. He looked exactly like Morgan, so much so that it made me wonder if our kids would look like that too.

We got to the car and Morgan got Indie settled in his car seat. He fell asleep almost instantly, and we drove off. A couple minutes into the drive, Morgan's phone automatically connected to the car's bluetooth and the text messages started flowing in, the automated system reading each one of them out loud.

"Katie, 11:56, I can't believe you're taking her on tour. This is ridiculous. She's a careless mom." Played on the car's speakers.

"What the fuck," Morgan said, checking his phone. I dug my nails into the palms of my hands.

"Katie, 11:58, I do not want that girl around my son. I have every right to say so."

"She's out of her fucking mind," he whispered. I turned around to make sure Indigo was still sleeping and couldn't hear what was going on.

"Katie, 12:00, I will not tolerate having a woman who mom-shamed me around Indie. Pick better girls or keep quietly fucking hoes, but don't bring this woman around my son. Period."

"Alright, that's enough," he said, disconnecting his phone from the bluetooth. "What the hell did you say to her?"

"Don't accuse me, she started it!" I defended myself.

"I'm not accusing you, I'm asking you."

"Well, I don't like your tone," I mumbled.

"Girl, will you please just tell me what the fuck happened?"

"She pulled me aside basically to tell me that I should hold off on letting you meet Ellie 'cause you were just gonna go on tour and cheat on me anyway, and that you always got super involved with women and messed it up the minute you left to go on tour-"

"She said that?!"

"Well, not verbatim, but pretty much," I summed up.

"That's fucked up."

"That's not even the fucked up part! I told her that I was actually going with you and she hit me with that 'Oh, well I guess we're different types of moms then, I could never leave Indie for that long'", I said, mimicking her. He chuckled.

"Please, tell me you didn't take that to heart."

"Well, no, but it still stung," I said. He squeezed my thigh gently.

"You're a good mom. You know that, and I know that. Don't let her get to you, she's just trying to mess with your head."

"Well, I kinda said something I'm not too proud of," I admitted. He raised an eyebrow, quietly asking me to go on. "I told her that we really were different types of moms because I'd never let my kid play with a big dog without surveillance," I mumbled. He covered his mouth, trying not to laugh.

"That's not cool," he said sternly while very obviously biting his cheeks to keep it together.

"She opened the door for me! What was I supposed to do?!"

"Baby, it's fine, but seriously, don't butt heads with her. It's not worth it," he stated. "She's the pettiest person I know and I don't want you to get dragged into her toxic bullshit. Just take the high road. Be the bigger person," he said softly.

"You're right, I shouldn't have said that. And I know she didn't do it on purpose, I mean, no mom would ever willingly let their child get hurt. I guess I just saw red when she attacked my parenting like that," I explained.

"And you had every right to. I'm just saying, for your own good, don't get sucked into her games. I'll call her when we get home and hash things out," he said. I gave him a funny look.

"I can call her in front of you if you want. Girl, if you think I still have any type of feelings for that girl, you are wildly fucking mistaken. I have absolutely nothing to hi-"

"It's fine, I didn't even say anything," I shrugged.

"Your eyes said plenty."

"Yeah? What did my eyes say?" I teased.

"That you're being a little jealous because you want me all to yourself," he winked. I scoffed and rolled my eyes. Cocky asshole.

Hi darlings! The number of views on this has gone up a fair amount in the last day so I'm super excited to see more people are embarking on this little adventure with us! I hope you guys like this. Thanks to every single one of you, every view/vote/comment matters!

XO

LadyBug

Chapter 17

We had spent the rest of the week at Morgan's parents' home where I had gotten to meet his entire family. Our kids had had time to bond, which I have to admit was pretty magical to watch. I had never really taken the time to imagine Ellie as a big sister, but seeing how caring she was towards Indigo truly made my heart melt. Katie had come to pick up Indie the night before we left to go on tour and Ellie was really sad to see him go. Even though Morgan had made it clear that he would not let her come between us, I had preferred to stay in our room when she had come to get her son. Our last encounter had left a bitter taste in my mouth and I was desperately trying to avoid another argument.

We had flown in from Knoxville to Milwaukee that morning, where Morgan was scheduled to play a sold out stadium that very night. I would be lying if I said that Ellie hadn't been on my mind the whole time; I'd never been so far away from her and the mom guilt was omnipresent. But, I tried, as much as I could, to take everything in and appreciate the moment because I knew this was a one of a kind experience and that tons of people would've killed to be in my shoes. It was about 3:00 PM when we got to the venue, just in time for the soundcheck. We had barely had time to set our stuff down before Morgan's manager, Seth, barged into his dressing room, instructing him to get on stage for the final soundcheck.

"They won't get off my back, man. I know the call sheet said 3:30 but apparently they need a break before the show, it's a union thing," Seth explained.

"That's alright, man. I'm here so might as well get this over with," Morgan said. "You can chill here if you want. It shouldn't take too long. Help yourself to anything you want, okay?" Morgan told me. I nodded and he placed a gentle kiss on my lips.

"Woah, guys, I'm not a snitch or anything, you don't have to do that here," Seth chuckled. I looked at Morgan and raised an eyebrow, confused by the comment. Morgan looked at him and subtly shook his head no.

"What?" I asked, genuinely confused.

"Nothing, baby. Old inside joke," he said, trying to brush it off.

"Okay," I said, still not fully grasping what they were going on about. Morgan gave me a quick kiss on the forehead and exited the room, followed by Seth, leaving me alone in the dressing room.

***

9:00 PM. The stadium was packed and the frenzy palpable. This guy named Hardy had just gone off the stage and Morgan was about to go on. The whole crowd was chanting his name and my heart was beating in my chest as if I was the one who had to go out there and put on a show for 40,000 people. Seth came to stand next to us and told Morgan he had 30 seconds until showtime. Morgan grabbed my face and spent twenty of those thirty seconds kissing me like no one else had ever kissed me. His lips softly mashed against mine, our bodies sharing one timeless, passionate moment. He pulled away gently and grazed my cheek softly with his thumb.

"I love you," he mouthed.

"I love you too," I replied before he gave me one last quick peck on the lips and ran on stage. The minute the spotlight hit him, the crowd went crazy. I bit my lip, almost as if I was nervous he'd mess up.

"Are you nervous?" Seth asked.

"Kinda," I admitted. "Probably not as much as him though," I giggled.

"Oh, he's used to it by now, but you're new to this. It's a very selfless thing you're doing, he's lucky you agreed," he smiled. I smiled back, slightly confused as to what he was referring to. "Don't worry, Jensen will come by tomorrow to coach you," he added.

"Coach me?" I asked.

"He's Morgan's publicist. He's the best, you'll see! This whole stunt was his idea, actually!"

"What stunt?" I asked, even more confused than before.

"Well, you know," he nudged me awkwardly. "The whole pretend relationship to make it make sense that he attacked your ex? At the baseball game? The whole thing was Jensen's idea. Brilliant guy! If it wasn't for him- and you might I add- I bet Morgan would've found himself in hot water. Again," he chuckled. "Pretty nice thing you're doing, especially with a kid in the mix and everything. I have mad respect for you, girl," he said, hitting my shoulder in a friendly way. "Anyway, I better go and do my job now! Enjoy the show, Aubrey!" he yelled, running off. I felt tears well up in my eyes. How could he do this to me? I looked at the first row of people. All women, screaming his name and reaching out their hands in hopes that he would touch them. How could I be this stupid? I left the backstage area, tears rolling down my face, and locked myself into his dressing room. I picked up my phone and immediately called Jared. It rang once before he picked up.

"Hey, girl! How are you liking the rockstar life?" he asked cheerfully.

"I want to come home, Jared. I can't stay here," I I cried, my breath trembling.

"What happened? Did he do something to you?"

"It's all a scam. He doesn't care about me, it's a PR strategy. Because of the Josh thing," I said, my heart breaking as I got the words out.

"Are you sure, Aubrey? That doesn't sound like h-"

"His manager told me."

"I'm gonna fucking kill him. Where are you right now?" he asked.

"In Milwaukee, locked into his dressing room." I sobbed quietly.

"Where's Ellie?"

"In Knoxville with his mom. I don't know what to do, Jared. I should have listened to you. And Chelsea. And even his fucking ex, everyone tried to warn me. I'm such a fucking idiot."

"You're not an idiot, Aubrey. He's a fucking piece of shit. I can't believe he fucking played you like that. If he's too much of an asshole to see how amazing a woman you are then that's on him. Not on you," he said. I sniffed.

"What do I do?" I asked, feeling completely and utterly gutted, stuck in a city I didn't know with people who wanted nothing more than to use me for their own benefit.

"Is Ernest there?" he asked.

"Yeah, he was playing earlier," I mumbled.

"Go see Ernest, put him on the phone for me," he requested.

"I can't, Jared. I'm so embarrassed, I don't want to face anyone right now."

"Aubrey, please let me help you. Go see Ernest, he's a good guy. I'll talk to him and I promise you he'll help you out."

"O-okay," I mumbled, unlocking the door. As I was leaving the room, I bumped into Ernest almost immediately.

"Hey, I saw you running off, I came to make sure you were okay," he said.

"Jared wants to talk to you," I said, passing him my phone.

"Okay?" he said, confused, putting the phone to his ear. "Hey, man, what's up?" he asked Jared. I couldn't hear what Jared was telling him, but Ernest furrowed his eyebrows. "That can't be right, you've heard him talk about her, ain't no way that-" he paused and looked at me. "Are you sure?" he asked me. I nodded. "Alright, Jared. I'll do what I can. Thanks, buddy," he said before hanging up and handing me back my phone.

"Aubrey, I'm not trying to be that guy, but I think you should wait and talk to him. I don't know what was said, but I do know Morgan and I've seen him around a lot of women. The way he looks at you is the same way I look at my wife. I genuinely think there's been a misunderstanding," he said calmly. I fucking knew he wouldn't help me. I felt tears well up in my eyes.

"This is too much for me, I want to go home. Please, help me get out of here," I begged. He sighed.

"Seth told you this?" He asked. I nodded. "There's no way that asshole will let you leave if he thinks you're his golden ticket. We'll have to go through the crowd to get you out," he said.

"Okay. Whatever you say, I trust you," I said, my voice cracking as I spoke. He gave me a faint smile. I could see in his eyes he felt bad for me. He didn't want me to leave, but he was a good man and his heart was in the right place. He was going to help me.

"There will be a lot of people trying to get to us, you'll have to hold my hand and push through people. We can't stop or we'll get trapped in the crowd. Do you understand?" He asked. I nodded.

"Alright, let's go," he said, swiftly opening the door that led us to the crowd. He started making his way through the sea of people, dragging me along with him.

"Oh my god, that's Ernest!" Someone said.

"Ernest, can we get a picture please!"

He ignored the requests, walking as fast as he could. We were almost out when I turned around and saw Morgan staring at me. Our eyes met for a second. He stopped signing, letting the crowd take over for him, his eyes not leaving mine. I could see the pain in his gaze. I could tell that he knew what was happening.

"C'mon, Aubrey," Ernest said, pulling me towards the exit. I turned around and got out of the venue, still holding Ernest's hand. As soon as the wind hit my face, I felt like I could breathe again.

"Thank you," I told Ernest, giving him a faint smile.

"Have Jared call me when you get home, okay?"

I nodded, giving him a quick hug before hailing a cab. I got into the car and closed the door, feeling my heart get heavier as I got further away from him.

"Where to, ma'am?" the driver asked.

"The airport."

So, apparently I hate Aubrey cause that poor girl can't seem to catch a break lmao

Hope y'all like this!

XO

LadyBug

Chapter 18

I sat in the airport, waiting to board the plane that would take me to Knoxville. I had left the venue over two hours ago and still had not gotten a single text from Morgan. I pulled out my phone to text Lesli and let her know I'd be coming to get Ellie.

AUBREY, 11:16 PM:

Hi Lesli, I know it's late, but something came up and I'll be flying to Knoxville to come get Ellie. I'm flying in tonight, but I'll come get her early tomorrow morning so that you don't have to stay up all night waiting for me. Thank you so much for taking care of Ellie while I was gone, I could only wish I had had a mom like you. xxx Aubrey

I put my phone back in my pocket and felt it buzzing against my skin almost immediately.

"Hello?" I picked up, expecting Lesli.

"I'm in a car, right outside the airport. Please, come out and we can talk," Morgan said, his voice breaking as he spoke.

"Who's phone is this?" I asked.

"Ernest's. I knew you wouldn't pick up if you saw my number calling so-"

"I'm not coming out, Morgan. Thank Ernest for everything and forget my number," I said, hanging up. I put my phone back into my pocket and felt it vibrating against my thigh again.

"What?!" I picked up impatiently.

"Is everything okay, darling?" Lesli asked. Shit.

"I am so sorry, I thought it was Mor-" I stopped myself from saying his name, realizing who I was speaking to. "I thought it was someone else."

"What's he done this time?" she asked.

"Can you be honest with me, Lesli?" I asked, my voice feeling as fragile as my heart.

"Sure, honey. Ask me anything."

"Did you know..?" I mumbled.

"Know what?" she asked.

"That he was using me to protect his image," I said, my voice breaking as I heard myself say these words out loud.

"What do you mean, using you to protect his image?"

"Because of the fight he had with my daughter's dad at the baseball game in Vermont," I admitted.

"That was your daughter's dad?!" she asked, seemingly shocked.

"I'm sorry, obviously you didn't know. I didn't mean to accuse you of anything or-"

"Oh, honey, don't apologize. Get on that plane and come home right away. None of that waiting until tomorrow morning bullcrap. I'll be up and I'll wait for you with a nice glass of whiskey and you can tell me what happened, alright?" she said softly.

"Okay, thank you," I said weakly, almost whispering, trying to swallow back tears.

"Just you wait, I'll give that kid a piece of my mind," she mumbled. I couldn't help but to giggle faintly. That woman was probably one of the nicest people I had met in my entire life. It pained me to think I would probably not get to see her again after this. "You travel safe, honey. Call me when you land," she said before hanging up. The flight attendant called everyone to board the plane. I grabbed my bag, and with a heavy heart, I walked to my seat.

***

I landed in Knoxville a couple of hours later. I remembered the last time I had been in that airport; the driver holding the "Mrs. Wallen" sign and the champagne in the car. I remembered how excited I was to see his face and to see how much effort he had put into decorating Ellie's room. I could still feel his skin against mine, his hands grabbing my waist and pulling me in for a kiss. His presence was haunting me. Following me as I made my way through the airport. I spotted a cab outside and hopped in. I gave the driver Lesli's address and he drove off into the night. I turned my phone back on. 7 texts and 4 missed calls. All from Morgan.

MORGAN, 11:30 PM:

Please, don't do this. It's not what you think, I swear. I know I should have told you about Jensen's plan but it didn't matter to me, that's why I didn't. I never meant to hurt you.

MORGAN, 11:46 PM:

Aubrey, I meant everything I said to you. None of this was a lie. You have to believe me.

MORGAN, 11:54 PM:

Baby, please come back. I love you...

MORGAN, 11:59 PM:

I know you love me too, please, Aubrey. Please, don't do this.

MORGAN, 12:11 AM:

I'll fucking fire Jensen if you come back, I don't care. Please, come back...

MORGAN, 12:46 AM:

Aubrey

MORGAN 1:06 AM:

Baby, please answer me...

I sighed.

AUBREY 3:07 AM:

You know what the worst part is? If you had just asked me to help you I probably would have. You didn't need to lie and play with my heart. And especially not with Ellie's heart. I can't believe you did this to me. Forget my number and leave me alone.

I hit send and shoved my phone back into my pocket, quickly closing my eyes, before it buzzed again.

MORGAN 3:11 AM:

You kniw I didm't fuckjng lie. You know I love yiu. You neber cared about mw.

He's drunk. Probably with some skinny blonde girl with perfect teeth and flawless skin. I bet she wears red lacy underwear. I turned off my phone and closed my eyes, trying to stop the tears from flowing. I was exhausted. I didn't even feel myself dozing off, but when I opened my eyes, the driver was pulling into the driveway of Lesli's house. She was waiting for me on the porch with two glasses and a bottle of Jack. I paid the driver and walked up to her.

"Hi," I mumbled. She smiled faintly and pulled me in for a hug, rubbing my back softly. I tried not to, but I couldn't help but to break down in her arms.

"Oh, honey. Let it out. It'll be okay," she comforted me softly.

"I'm sorry," I mumbled into her shoulder.

"Don't apologize, darling. You did nothing wrong. You're home now." she said, kissing the side of my head like a mother would her daughter. I wiped my tears and pulled away from the hug. Lesli poured me a glass of whiskey and handed it to me.

"There, honey. Now tell me what happened. From the beginning."

This is a short chapter, but hopefully you guys don't hate me too much for the turn things took and still want to read this!! Some more drama coming!

XO

LadyBud

Chapter 19

Lesli and I had gone to bed late last, talking about what had happened with Morgan. She seemed to be as disappointed as I was and had assured me that no matter what happened between him and I, Ellie and I would always be welcome at her house. She had made me promise, before dropping us off at the airport, that I would still let Ellie call her grandma Lesli and that she would FaceTime her every once in a while. I was sad to leave. My heart was in pieces and I didn't know how long it would take until I would be able to glue it back together. I'd had high hopes for Morgan and I's relationship, to a point where I let my feelings cloud my judgment. I had made poor choices over the last few weeks and I desperately needed to go home and get back to my normal life in order to correct things. Morgan had sent me a few texts, saying he was sorry, again, and that I should call him, which I hadn't done and didn't plan on doing.

"I thought we'd be staying here longer, mama," Ellie said, pulling me from my thoughts.

"Me too, baby. Sometimes, things don't turn out the way we plan."

"I'm gonna miss Grandma Lesli," she pouted.

"I know, baby. I'm gonna miss her too, I admitted.

"When is Morgan coming home, mama?" she asked. I felt my heart sink into my chest.

"I don't think Morgan will be around anymore, Ellie," I explained.

"Why?" she asked.

"Sometimes, when people don't treat us right, we have to walk away and protect ourselves," I said, squeezing her little shoulder gently.

"Like we did with daddy?" she asked. My heart broke at that question. That little girl had already been through so much. And the worst part was that he knew that and still was careless. I didn't know how I could ever forgive him for that. Or myself, frankly.

****

We landed in Burlington at around 4:00 PM and took a cab ride to Jared's house. He had made me promise that we would come see him as soon as we landed, so we did. Ellie rang the doorbell and he opened the door right away.

"Why, if this isn't princess Eleanor! Please come in, milady," he said, bowing down to her jokingly.

"You're funny," she giggled, walking into the house. "Can I watch Cocomelon?"

"You can do whatever you want princess," he answered. I heard her little footsteps run towards the living room and turn the TV on.

"I'm sorry," I whispered, feeling my eyes well up with tears.

"Stop apologizing, you did nothing wrong," he said, pulling me in for a hug.

"I should have listened to you," I whispered into his neck.

"Live and learn," he said, rubbing my back softly. "Live and learn."

I pulled away from the hug and walked into the house, closing the front door behind me.

"Has he tried to contact you?"

"Only a million times," I exaggerated.

"Have you given him the chance to explain?"

"Explain what. Seems pretty simple to me," I snapped.

"Alright, don't get mad at me. I was just asking," he said softly.

"Sorry, I just- I don't feel too good," I apologized.

"That's alright, did you eat today?" he asked. I shook my head no. "Well, that can't help. Let me whip you up something."

"Don't bother, I don't think I can stomach anything right now."

"How come?"

"I don't know, I've been super nauseous today. Probably just the lack of sleep, mixed in with the roller coaster of emotions," I explained.

"If you say so," he said. "If you think you caught some sort of bug or something, maybe you shouldn't come back to work right away, though."

"I'm fine, Jared. I'm just tired."

"Go lie down," he said.

"I'll be alright, really-"

"Go lay down, Aubrey. I'll watch Ellie," he insisted.

"Really?" I asked.

"Go!"

***

I woke up a few hours later, in Jared's bed, with my stomach in my throat. I got out of bed slowly and the nausea increasingly got worse. I clutched my stomach and made my way to the bathroom quietly. Jared saw me emerging from the bedroom.

"Hey, did you sleep well?" he asked. I nodded and gave him a thumbs up, unable to speak, fearing I would throw up all over his floor if I did.

"Are you good?" he asked. I ignored his question and ran to the bathroom, knowing full well I couldn't keep it in much longer. I slammed the door behind me and gagged, emptying the contents of my stomach into the toilet. Jared came in a few seconds after me and held my hair as I kept retching.

"I don't want you to see me like this," I mumbled into the toilet bowl.

"I'm a doctor, trust me, I've seen worse," he joked. "Here," he said, handing me a glass of water. I took the water and flushed the vile soup of meals past down the toilet. I sat on the floor, sipping slowly from the glass of water.

"So, are we gonna talk about it?" he asked.

"Talk about what?" I breathed, exhausted.

"Aubrey," he insisted.

"What?" I snapped, not getting the subtlety of his message.

"I don't think the emotions are what's making you sick, or what made you take an eight hour nap at 4 o'clock in the afternoon," he stated.

"I slept for eight hours?! Shit, what time is it? Where's Ellie?"

"It's a little past midnight. Ellie's sleeping in the guest room," he said.

"I'm so sorry, I'm just exhausted."

"And nauseous," he added. "And unable to stomach anything," he said, tilting his head slightly.

"No, that's not what this is," I assured him.

"Well, have you taken a test? 'Cause I know you weren't on the pill, he called me to-"

"I'm not pregnant, Jared!" I snapped.

"Brey," he said softly. "If you are, ignoring it won't make it go away."

I didn't know what to say. I wanted to yell at him and scream and cry and punch a hole in the freaking wall, but none of that would have mattered. I could keep my head in the sand for as long as I wanted, but the truth was; I knew he was right. I hadn't felt that way since I had first gotten pregnant with Ellie. My head started spinning.

"It's still early, you know. You have options," he said.

"No, Jared! No, I don't! Maybe some women do and I respect that but I do not. I don't want to even thin-"

"Okay," he said softly. "You don't have to yell, or get angry. I'm just saying that whatever you do, I'll be by your side," he explained, taking my hand into his.

"Can I ask you one favor," I said, my eyes welling up with tears.

"Anything you want."

"Please, don't tell him."

Chapter 20

A little over 11 weeks had passed since I had last seen Morgan and I was now 14 weeks pregnant. Jared had been doing my check ups, but still told me frequently he disagreed with my choice of not telling Morgan. I could see why he would feel that way but I genuinely didn't think neither Morgan, nor I, had anything to gain from him knowing about the pregnancy. Two kids from two different women, none of which he was dating, would probably do quite the number on his reputation- which I now knew for a fact he would do anything to protect. And what was in it for me? Money? Fame? It's not like I wanted either of those things. I was determined not to take a penny from him. I would swallow my pride for a lot of things, but not that. Absolutely not. And being a mom was hard enough as it was, I had no interest in doing it in the public eye with hoards of people criticizing my every move. I realized that I might have judged Katie a bit hastily. After all, she knew Morgan, and had tried to warn me and protect Ellie. I had stumbled upon online articles about Indie's dog attack and people were being insanely harsh towards her. I genuinely felt bad for her and regretted my comment. I had thought of writing her to apologize, but couldn't bring myself to do it. Some new pictures of Morgan with a mystery blonde girl, sharing a kiss on his front porch a couple weeks after I had left, had surfaced online. I would be lying if I said that didn't break my heart a little more. To know he had already moved on from us was a hard pill to swallow. But he had every right to live his life and even though it stung, I couldn't hold that against him. We didn't owe each other anything and that was fine.

Ellie had been facetiming Lesli every week since we had gotten back from Tennessee and I had done a pretty good job at hiding the pregnancy from her too. But the more time passed, the more apparent the baby bump started to become.

I layed down in bed, dreading work in the morning. The nausea had gotten better, which I was grateful for, but my energy levels were still way off. Thankfully, Jared had been, once again, the most understanding and empathetic boss I could have ever asked for. I was scrolling down my Facebook feed when I noticed a text from Chelsea.

CHELSEA, 9:37 PM:

I think he's talking about you, dude!!! *hyperlink*

I clicked on the link and it led me to a TikTok that had been recorded by a fan during one of Morgan's concerts. You could see him, sitting at the piano, wearing that white long-sleeved shirt that I liked so much on him. My heart skipped a beat when he started speaking. I turned the volume up.

"A little while ago, I met an amazing lady," he started, the crowd already going wild. "The kind of lady that makes you want to stop messing around and settle down for good. And then I messed things up, making her feel like she didn't matter to me. Aubrey, wherever you are, if you see this; I wrote this song for you," he said, before letting his fingers run softly over the keys. He started singing and the words sent shivers down my spine.

"Girl, since you left me

Been tryin' to forget we

Ever became what we were

And I poured some whiskey

On places you kissed me

Tried to wash off all the hurt

But ain't nothin' workin'

I've lived out the words in

A thousand old sad country songs

But whenever I try to move on

It's like tryna put a Band-Aid on a bullet hole

Tryna tell a cowboy to slow down

It's like watchin' the way that the river rolls

And then tellin' it to turn back around

And I've held some strangers, told people I hate you

But I just keep hittin' a wall

It's like tryna put a Band-Aid on a bullet hole

It just don't do me no good at all

If I was only

Heartbroke and lonely

I'd head on back down to the bar

Find me a companion

But you left a canyon

Can't nobody fill in this heart

And girl, it's like tryna put a Band-Aid on a bullet hole

Tryna tell a cowboy to slow down

It's like watchin' the way that the river rolls

And then tellin' it to turn back around

And I've held some strangers, told people I hate you

But I just keep hittin' a wall

It's like tryna put a Band-Aid on a bullet hole

It just don't do me no good at all

No damn good, damn good, damn good at all

And baby, tell me how you did it?

I just gotta know

And tell me what's your secret?

And how'd you let me go so easy?

'Cause girl, it's like tryna put a Band-Aid on a bullet hole

Tryna tell a cowboy to slow down

It's like watchin' the way that the river rolls

And then tellin' it to turn back around

Oh, I've held some strangers, told people I hate you

But I just keep hittin' a wall

It's like tryna put a Band-Aid on a bullet hole

It just don't do me no good at all

It's like tryna put a Band-Aid on a bullet hole

It just don't do me no good at all

No damn good, damn good, damn good at all"

I looked at the date on the video. It had been recorded the night before, at his Tacoma show; the last show on his tour. I felt my eyes well up with tears. I couldn't believe what I had just seen. Maybe he really had been telling the truth? But that's irrelevant. It's too late, right? My mind was racing. I heard my phone buzzing against the throw blanket that was on my bed, pulling me out of my thoughts.

"Hello?"

"He wrote a song about you, you know," Jared sighed.

"I know, Chelsea just sent me the video," I mumbled.

"It's not fair what you're doing to him, Aubrey."

"What I am doing to him?" I asked, offended. "Do I have to remind you of why things are the way that they are? He played me, Jared! I was all in! I had uprooted my daughter's life for him, left my job and my apartment behind to follow him around the fucking country! And he used me!"

"You never even heard him out. And now you're carrying his child and he doesn't even know. You're my best friend, Aubrey. You are, but he's my friend too and I can't keep lying to him when I know it's not right."

"I can't believe you're gonna do me like that, Jared. Seriously?! You know having two kids from two baby mamas is gonna mess up his reputation! What could he possibly have to gain from that?"

"He doesn't care about his reputation! He never fucking did! Do you see the way he conducts himself?! You think this guy gives two-shits about what his dumb fucking publicist has to say?" he asked, audibly irritated. He took a deep breath in and exhaled slowly, trying to regulate his emotions. "I know Morgan, Aubrey. I've known him since we were five years old and if there's one thing I'm sure of, it's that he's gonna want to meet his child. You don't get to take that away from him. If you don't tell him, I will," he said sternly before hanging up on me. Who the fuck does he think he is?! I threw my phone angrily, accidently hitting the lamp on my nightstand with it, which fell on the floor and exploded into a hundred little ceramic pieces.

"Fuck!' I yelled, slamming my fist into the mattress. I got off the bed and made my way to the kitchen to get the broom when I heard a knock on the door. I glanced at the clock on the kitchen wall; 10:12 PM. What the fuck? I looked through the peephole to see who was there and I froze. This can't be right. I opened the door slowly, poking my head out.

"Please, don't close the door," Morgan said, his voice weak.

"Why are you here?" I asked.

"I played my last show of the tour last night," he mumbled.

"I know. That's not what I asked. Why are you here?"

"I needed to see you," he admitted.

"Why? Is your publicist here to coach me too?" I snapped.

"Aubrey, you have to believe me, that was never what that was about," he sighed. "I loved you, hell I still do."

"So, why are you here, Morgan?" I asked, ignoring his confession.

"Because I want to fix things. I'm done touring for at least a year now. Maybe I'll still do a show here and there but I'm done being on the road for a while. I have all the time in the world to focus on you and Ellie and I want to prove to you that I'm serious," he said. "Can I please come in?" he mumbled.

"I don't know, I don't think that's a good idea-"

"Please let me hold you," he said, his voice breaking. "I know I fucked up, but I need you in my arms right now, baby. Please."

I hesitated for a second. His eyes looked so sincere, but I had been fooled before. But, seeing him so fragile, so raw, asking me for a second chance, made me want to hold him too. I looked into his eyes. Those damn blue eyes that had made me fall for him in the first place. Those same blue eyes that made me let him in that night.

I opened the door, finally allowing him to come inside, but he froze. As soon as he saw my whole body, his eyes immediately traveled to the little baby bump that was making my shirt a whole lot tighter than it was three months ago. Shit.

"Are you... pregnant?"

So we hit 1k views today which is really awesome!! Thanks to everyone reading/voting/commenting! Your feedback truly means the world to me!

XO

LadyBug

Chapter 21

"Are you... Pregnant?" he asked, not taking his eyes off me. I grabbed the sweater that was hung behind the door and put it on quickly, forcing him to stop looking at the baby bump. He looked deep into my eyes before repeating the question.

"Aubrey, are you?" he asked, again. I nodded.

"Is it mine?" I nodded again. He grinned for a second before his eyes turned dark.

"So, what? Were you just not gonna tell me?!" he asked, obviously agitated. "That's fucked up."

"I didn't think you'd gain anything from knowing. It'll just mess up your reputation and-"

"Don't you think that's up to me to decide?" he snapped, obviously shocked by the news.

"Like you've never hidden anything from me."

"This is different! How the fuck could you do this to me? Fucking hide a kid from me, Aubrey?! Did you think I wasn't gonna find out? That Jared wasn't gonna find-" he stopped himself mid sentence before realizing what was happening. "Jared fucking knew didn't he?!"

"Morgan, it's not like th-"

"I can't believe he fucking knew and didn't tell me," he laughed dryly, rubbing the back of his neck. "What was the plan here? Y'all were just gonna play house with my kid?!"

"He wanted me to tell you, he did. But-"

"But what, Aubrey?"

"But I didn't want to, okay?!" I snapped.

"You hate me that much, huh?" he said, visibly hurt by my previous statement.

"I hate the way you used me and made me feel this fucking small," I said, bringing my thumb and index finger close together. "I hate the way you were caught kissing some random blonde on your front porch a mere two weeks after I left! I hate that you made Ellie cry when she realized you really weren't coming back and how you made me fall in love with you just to watch me fall apart! I don't hate you, Morgan. I wish I did, but I don't. But I hate the way you've treated me and I thought, you know what? I'd rather go through this alone than with someone who doesn't care about me," I snapped.

"I should have been honest with you, granted. But telling me I don't care about you? That's a lie and you know that. You wanna villainize every little thing I do? Fine. But, You left. You ignored my texts and my calls for weeks on end and what? Now you want to blame me because I fucked a random girl four weeks after you left, by the way. Not two, four. And you wanna know why I know that? Because I sent you 28 fucking texts telling you I loved you. I sent you one everyday, for four weeks, because I'd made you a promise the first time I told you I loved you, that I'd tell you everyday for the rest of my life. And I did that for four fucking weeks without getting nothing back from you, not a fuck you, no nothing. So yeah, I thought fuck it, I need to get her out of my system. And yeah, the girl from the pictures my asshole neighbor took? Yeah, I fucked her, Aubrey. I did," he chuckled dryly. "And you know what? That didn't change a fucking thing. I still woke up the next day with her in my bed wishing she was you. But you don't get to fucking weaponize that. Not when I'd just spent a fucking month begging you to give me the time of day. That's not fair." he spat angrily. My head started spinning.

"I need to sit down," I sighed, pulling out a chair from under the kitchen table.

"Are you okay?" he asked, genuinely concerned.

"I'm just dizzy," I said. He sat on the chair next to me.

"I don't wanna fight with you, that's not why I came here," he said gently, pulling his chair closer to mine and taking my hand into his. "I just wish you would've told me. I have a right to know these things."

"I should have, I know. And I was going to, but then I saw you with that girl and I thought maybe you were happy with someone else and that I shouldn-"

"Marry me," he interrupted.

"What?" My eyes widened, shocked by what he had just said.

"I'm serious, let's get married. And we can have a big wedding and plaster it all over social media and everyone will know we're married. You're never gonna have to worry about another girl ever again, no one will want to fuck the married guy," he chuckled and I bursted out laughing.

"I think you're overestimating the girl code a little bit," I laughed. "Look, there are gonna be girls who want to be with you and who hang out around you and that's not gonna stop. I have to figure out a way to deal with it and how it affects me and rushing into marriage is not the solution."

"Just say you don't wanna marry me, at this point," he pouted. I giggled.

"You're annoying. And a little bit crazy," I teased.

"Girl, shut up and admit you missed me already," he said, getting up from his chair and pulling on my hand for me to get up too. I got on my feet and he pushed me slightly, sitting me up on the kitchen table. He put his hands on my waist, and got closer to me, spreading my legs slightly, my thighs now resting on either side of him. He looked into my eyes softly, making my heart beat speed up.

"I missed you," I admitted.

"I love you," he whispered, his eyes not leaving mine.

"I love you too," I mumbled. He placed his hand on the back of my neck and pulled me in for a kiss, his lips parting slowly to let his tongue dance with mine. The warmth of his breath tickled my nose and his hands ran slowly over my body, stopping abruptly on my stomach. He pulled away from the kiss softly and looked down at my bump, placing his hands on it softly.

"Do you know if it's a boy or a girl?" he asked.

"Not yet, four more weeks until the anatomy scan. We'll find out then," I smiled faintly.

"Can I... be there?"

"If you want," I said. He beamed, still staring at my stomach, his hands not leaving it.

"I never got to do that with Indie, you know. Katie and I were already broken up and butting heads and she didn't really want me around during her pregnancy. I hate that I missed that. I want to be here this time. Take care of you, both of you," he said softly.

"You're a good guy," I admitted.

"I don't know about that. But I want to be, for you and Ellie... and the baby," he said softly. "I can't believe I'm gonna be a dad again," he whispered looking into my eyes.

"You know I'm not trying to trap you, right? 'Cause I know you said that Katie- And I don't want your money, I-"

"Aubrey," he said, putting an end to my rambling. I sighed. "You could drain my fucking bank account for all I care. You're not trapping me into anything. I know we didn't plan this, but I couldn't think of a better mom for my kid. I'm happy. Really happy," he said, placing a soft kiss on my forehead. I smiled.

"Really?" I asked.

"Really," he said gently, giving me a little nod.

"MORGAAN!!" Ellie yelled, running from her bedroom and hugging his leg. He chuckled.

"Hi, Miss Ellie. Did you take good care of your mama for me?" he asked. She nodded.

"What are you doing up, El? It's late," I told her.

"I heard Morgan and I wanted to say hi," she beamed at him, completely ignoring me. "Does this mean we get to go back to grandma Lesli's house?" she asked, excited.

"Yes," Morgan said at the exact same time as I said "No." We looked at each other and I frowned.

"We'll see, El. Now go back to bed, honey, it's late," I instructed her. She frowned and stomped her little foot.

"C'mon, baby. I'll tuck you in," Morgan said, walking her to her bedroom. And for a second, all was right with the world.

Don't get fooled, if you know me at all by now, you know I got some more drama coming your way!

Thanks for the support, you guys! I have a bit of a busy week this week, but I will try to update at the very least daily (and more if I can)!

XO

LadyBug

Chapter 22

Morgan got out of Ellie's room, closing the door quietly behind him.

"She was fast asleep," he whispered, making his way to the kitchen where I was snacking directly out of the fridge. "Some water with that, Winnie The Pooh?" he joked, pointing at the red t-shirt I was wearing that was now a little too tight to reach the end of my stomach. I pulled on it slightly, trying to cover myself up and he laughed at my fruitless efforts.

"I'm so hungry, you don't understand," I complained. "I was the same way with Ellie." He laughed.

"It looks good on you," he said, kissing the top of my head.

"What does?"

"The little baby bump, probably even more efficient than a wedding ring," he joked.

"You're a dick," I rolled my eyes, giggling.

"Hey, I offered the wedding too! You didn't want it," he chuckled.

"Yeah, not like that! Hey girl, let's get married so you stop being jealous of them other hoes," I said in his accent, jokingly. "How romantic."

"So, does that mean that if I make it romantic you'll say yes?" he asked. I felt my cheeks flare up.

"I don't know, I guess we'll see," I said, shrugging shyly. He smiled.

"Hey why did you tell Ellie we couldn't go to my mom's house?" he asked, changing the subject.

"I mean, we can go visit her, but I don't think that's what she was asking."

"But you do plan on moving to Tennessee, right?"

"In your fucking frat house? Yeah, I don't think so."

"We can sell the house and buy a new one, Aubrey. It's not about the house," he said.

"I like Vermont, my life is here."

"I have a kid in Tennessee!"

"And I have a kid in Vermont!" I said in the same tone.

"It's not the same thing, you know that," he said, dismissing my comment. I raised my eyebrows and tilted my head, warning him to tread lightly.

"And why exactly is that?"

"Because she doesn't have a dad! You get to move away, I don't!"

"Wow, I can't believe you just said that. You're an asshole," I mumbled.

"No, that's not- You know what I mean," he said defensively. "You can't expect me to be a full time parent to two kids who live 11 hours away from one another!"

"Frankly, I don't expect anything from you, Morgan," I said dryly.

"That's not fair," he said as I started walking towards my bedroom. He grabbed my forearm semi-roughly and pulled me back in his direction. "Stop!," he said, aggravated. "Stop running away from me! Every time we have a disagreement you shut me out! Why do you keep doing that?! Why can't we just talk and compromise like normal people?!"

"Because everyone in my life has fucking failed me, Morgan! My mom abandoned me and my dad died, and even Josh bailed on Ellie and I as soon as he got the chance! You want me to blindly jump into this crazy adventure with you! Drive into the sunset and never look back! Well, I can't do that! I don't trust you," I admitted, feeling tears well up in my eyes. He sighed.

"You don't have to fucking yell at me, Aubrey. I'm not def," he snapped.

"You've been here an hour and we're already fighting," I sighed. "This is exactly what I mean. What if I move across the country for you and we just end up fighting all the time? What then?" I said, my voice breaking. He took my hand into his and gently stroked it with his thumb, exhaling slowly.

"You're upset, and hormonal, and that's normal. I'm not trying to fight with you," he said softly. I looked down, trying to hide the tears that were rolling down my cheeks. "Do you want me to leave?" he asked. I shook my head no and he sighed, kissing the top of my head gently.

"I know you don't trust me, I get it," he continued. "I'm going to do everything I can to change that, but can you please just be open minded?" he asked.

"In what way?"

"Come look at houses in Nash' with me. Maybe there will be one you like. And if you don't, I won't twist your arm. But, either way, I want you to feel comfortable at my house and right now I know that you don't. Would that be a good start? And we can take it from there," he suggested. I nodded faintly. "Just talk to me when something's wrong, Aubrey. I'm on your team, you don't have to be so guarded with me."

"I'm just trying to keep Ellie safe and happy," I admitted. "I don't want her childhood to be unstable and messed up like mine."

"And rightfully so, but it won't be, I promise. Plus, I sincerely think that little girl likes me more than you do," he chuckled. I sniffed, wiping my eyes softly and giggled.

"She really does like you," I admitted.

I heard my phone vibrating against the kitchen table, cutting our conversation short.

"Hello?" I picked up

"Have you given what I said any more thought?" Jared asked.

"I told him," I said. "He knows I'm pregnant."

"Is that Jared?" Morgan asked. I nodded. "Put him on speaker phone," he requested and I obliged.

"Hey, Jared?" Morgan asked.

"Morg- Are you guys together? Are you in Vermont?" Jared babbled, seemingly confused.

"Yeah, I'm in Vermont, buddy. I just wanted to let you know that your secretary will not be coming into work anymore," Morgan said.

"Excuse me?!" I asked. He winked at me.

"You owe me one for, you know, harboring a fugitive," Morgan added.

"What do you mean?" Jared asked.

"You let my pregnant girlfriend hide under your skirt, asshole," he joked.

"Aubrey, you told him that I knew?! Not cool!" Jared said. This phonecall is fucking chaos. "Fine, whatever you need," Jared said before quickly hanging up.

"What the fuck was that about?" I asked.

"I told you I was gonna take care of you. There's no way I'm gonna let my pregnant girlfriend kill herself at work. Especially considering she doesn't need to. Now go get undressed, I'm drawing you a bath," he ordered.

"So bossy," I said, walking towards my room to get undressed.

"You're welcome!" He yelled jokingly as I walked away.

This is super short and fairly uneventful but I felt like it might help the readers understand Aubrey's reactions a little better! Let me know what you guys think or what you would like to see happen over the next chapters!

XO

LadyBug

Chapter 23

Morgan had spent the rest of that night on the phone with a realtor, demanding the world in a 48 hour window. He had all these insane criterias for the new house and had his mind set on buying it this week.

"You do understand that what you're asking for is a little bit crazy, right?" I had asked, my head resting on his chest and my eyelids already feeling heavy.

"She's supposed to be the best realtor in Nashville! Surely, she can make it happen," he argued. I giggled. "We're gonna go to my mom's tomorrow, and then go to Nash the next day and spend the whole day looking at houses and I'm sure you'll find your pick," he whispered into my ear.

"Whatever you want," I yawned. He kissed the top of my head, pulling me in even closer.

"You smell good," I mumbled, slowly falling asleep. He chuckled softly.

"Alright, go to sleep, mama."

***

The flight to Knoxville had gone fairly smoothly. Ellie had been asleep through most of it and Morgan had used the time to show me some of the -very overpriced- houses that the realtor had sent him, to get an idea of what I liked. We got off the plane and made our way to the baggage claim.

"I'm so happy you're here," Morgan said, kissing the top of my head gently. I smiled.

"Oh my god," I heard someone whisper behind me. I turned around and noticed two girls in their early twenties were standing behind us, staring at him. "Morgan, can we get a picture?" One of them asked.

"Sure," he said nonchalantly. They ran towards him and one of them bumped into Ellie, making her fall over. She started crying and I picked her up, staring angrily at the girl.

"Can you watch where you're going?" I snapped. Morgan squeezed my hand gently.

"Don't push my kid over y'all. You'll get your picture, but be respectful," he said calmly.

"That's Indie?" The girl asked. Why the fuck do they know his whole life like that?

"No, that's not- We're in a bit of a hurry, guys."

"Sorry," they apologized quickly. "Can we make a TikTok? Can you sing?" They asked, pulling out their phones. He took a quick picture with them and other people seemed to notice the commotion because before I knew it we were surrounded by people asking for pictures and shoving Ellie and I left and right. I saw our luggage come out on the carousel and tried to pick it up by myself.

"No heavy lifting ma'am," Morgan teased, doing it for me.

"Oh my god, are you expecting another baby, Morgan?" Some girl asked.

"Can we get a picture? It'll only take a second!" Another one begged.

He picked up Ellie, putting her on his hip and held my hand, guiding us through the crowd.

"Morgan, I love you!" This girl screamed right in my ear. I turned around and stared at her. What the fuck is wrong with these people?! "Just one picture, please!"

"Not today, guys! Sorry, I hope y'all have a great day," he said calmly, smiling at his fans who were following us through the airport. Jesus H. Christ, he's not a circus animal. These people are so freaking intense.

We got to the pick up spot where a driver was supposed to be waiting for us. I recognized him immediately.

"Andrew!" I smiled.

"Mrs. Wallen, Ms. Ellie," he said, nodding his head politely before opening the door for us. I giggled. Morgan got in after us and Andrew closed the door and went to put the luggage in the trunk. I sighed, feeling like I could finally breathe.

"You okay?" Morgan asked.

"That was a lot," I admitted.

"You'll get used to it," he said, kissing the top of my head gently. Andrew got in the car and we drove away from the crowded airport.

"Andrew, do you have any snacks?" I said, quietly fighting nausea.

"Of course, Mrs. Wallen," he answered, handing me a cute little basket filled with snacks.

"I told you, please, call me Aubrey," I said, taking the basket.

"I like Mrs. Wallen, I think it has a nice ring to it," Morgan said, winking at me. "What do you think, Andrew?"

"Sure does, Mr. Wallen," he answered politely. I rolled my eyes.

"Don't drag him into your antics," I said, defending poor Andrew. Morgan chuckled.

The rest of the drive went by quickly and before I realized it, Andrew was pulling into the driveway leading to Lesli's house. We got out of the car and Morgan got Ellie out of her carseat, carrying her to the house.

"Hi, mom!" Morgan yelled as we walked in.

"Morgan Cole Wallen," Lesli yelled from the otherside of the house. "You have some nerve! Bringing home the perfect woman to screw it all up in the span of a week?! I don't know what I have done to the Lord to-" she stopped speaking as soon as her eyes met mine.

"Hi, Lesli," I smiled.

"Grandma Lesli!!" Ellie yelled, running into her arms.

"Hi, baby," Lesi said, picking her up and covering her face in little kisses. She turned back to me.

"Oh, honey! Isn't this the best surprise," she said, pulling me in for a hug. "I am so happy that you found it in your heart to forgive my idiotic son," she joked, slapping the back of Morgan's head.

"Hey!" he complained. I giggled.

"Aren't you stunning? You look like you're glowing," she complimented, smiling at me.

"Thank you," I mumbled shyly.

"You don't notice anything?" Morgan asked her. She looked at him confused.

"It's still early, it doesn't really show when I have a sweater on," I told him. She opened her mouth and quickly covered it with her hand.

"No way! Aubrey, don't let him mess with me like that," she said, tearing up. "Are you for real?!" she asked. I nodded and smiled at her. "I'm gonna be a grandma again?"

"You're gonna be a grandma again," Morgan confirmed. She quickly wiped the tears of joy streaming down her face.

"Does that mean you're gonna move here, honey?" she asked, obviously excited.

"Well, nothing's set in stone yet, but we are going to go look at houses in Nashville tomorrow," I smiled.

"Oh, I need to sit down," she said, putting her hand on her chest. "You two kids are gon' give me a heart attack," she joked, putting Ellie down and catching her breath. Morgan chuckled. "Oh, stop laughing, you. You got lucky," she told him, slapping his shoulder playfully. "Has he been treating you well?" She asked me. I nodded, giggling.

"Like a princess, I swear," I smiled

"Good. That's how pregnant women should be treated."

"I'm buying her a house!" He said, defending himself.

"You oughta buy her a ring too," she said, creating a slightly awkward silence.

"Where's Boots?" He asked, looking around for his dog, which I secretly thought was to save me from an awkward conversation.

"Dad took her hunting with him," she replied.

"Couldn't wait for me?"

"Boy, you got some nerves. Didn't even call before showing up and now you're complaining that he's gone hunting without you?" He chuckled and I yawned.

"Are you tired, baby?" He asked softly.

"Kind of," I said. "All this moving around got to me."

"Go lay down," he said gently. "I'll watch Ellie."

"Are you sure?" I asked. He nodded and gave me a gentle peck on the lips. I smiled and thanked him quickly before heading to his room and laying down on the king size bed. I checked my phone quickly and opened my facebook. The first thing I saw on my feed sent shivers down my spine.

"Country Singer Morgan Wallen Spotted Traveling With Pregnant Girlfriend a Few Weeks After Being Caught Kissing Mystery Girl In Front of His Nashville Home"

I hope you all had a blessed day!

XO

LadyBug

Chapter 24

"Country Singer Morgan Wallen Spotted Traveling With Pregnant Girlfriend a Few Weeks After Being Caught Kissing Mystery Girl In Front of His Nashville Home"

I clicked on the link and realized they had not only posted pictures of Morgan and I, but ones of Ellie too. My blood was boiling. Who the fuck did these people think they were, posting pictures of my three year old daughter for everyone to see. I jumped out of bed, the sleepiness having completely left my body by now.

"Morgan!" I yelled walking down the hallway. "Look at this!" I said, pulling out my phone to show him. He looked at me, scared of what I was about to show him. He took my phone in his hand and looked at the screen.

"Well, that was fast," he said, sounding almost unbothered. He handed my phone back to me.

"What the fuck?!" I asked.

"Baby, obviously people were gonna find out. I didn't think it would be this fast, but, hey. What can you do?" He shrugged.

"They got pictures of Ellie! That's fucked up!" I said, obviously agitated.

"Wait, they did?" He finally reacted, grabbing my phone from my hand and taking a second look at the pictures. "Oh, hell nah," he said, handing me back my phone and getting off the couch. He pulled out his phone and put it up to his ear.

"Who are you calling?"

"Seth," he said. "Hey man, did you see the article?" he asked him. "They posted pictures of my stepdaughter, didn't even bother to blur her face. Can we find out who posted this? This needs to go down like yesterday," he said, waiting for Seth's answer. I couldn't make out what he was telling Morgan, but I could feel my heart was about to burst out of my chest. I had signed up for this, granted. I knew who Mogan was, I knew his life was very public and I still had made the choice to be a part of it. But Ellie had nothing to do with that. She had made no choice of her own and she had every right to have her privacy respected. "Thanks, man. Call me as soon as you have news, alright?" Morgan told Seth before hanging up.

"So?" I asked impatiently.

"He's already on it. He says this actually came from a subreddit, posted from a throwaway account. He has someone trying to track it down right now," he said, taking my hand into his. "Don't worry, I will take care of this. I promise," he said, looking deep into my eyes.

"I just can't believe people would stoop that low. She's a little kid for God's sake," I sighed, genuinely discouraged.

"These scumbags will do anything to make a buck on other people's backs. Don't let that shit get to you. I swear it will be gone by tonight," he said softly, kissing the top of my head.

I sat down on the couch next to him and waited. Every passing second felt like an hour. The phone wasn't ringing and I was starting to lose hope that we'd be able to get these pictures taken down in time to limit the damage.

I did not want my daughter's face plastered all over social media. I didn't want her to know how cruel people could be online. She did not need the judgment of others passed onto her, especially not at three years old. I was looking at Ellie who was quietly playing with her toys. At least she had no idea of what was happening. My anxiety levels were through the roof, wondering how we would ever be able to fix this. I could feel tears starting to well up in my eyes when the phone finally rang. Morgan picked up right away.

"Hey man, lay it on me," he said, putting his cell on speakerphone so I could hear what was happening.

"So we were able to locate the IP address and match it to an actual street address. It seems to be coming from this condo in Nashville. I'll send the location to you to see if you recognize it. Now let me make myself clear, Morgan; it is not an invitation to go down there. Do you understand me?" Seth asked. Morgan looked at me quickly, as to see if I was agreeing with Seth.

"Alright," he mumbled.

"Okay I just texted you the address, does it ring a bell?" Seth asked. Morgan looked at his phone and scratched the back of his head.

"Not really, no," he said perplexed.

"Alright, I'll have someone try and contact them ASAP."

"Alright, thanks man," Morgan said before hanging up. "Ma' can you watch Ellie for a couple hours?" he asked.

"Why?" I inquired.

"We're gonna go talk to them."

"But Seth said-"

"I don't give a shit what Seth said, no one gets turn my step-daughter into a fucking profit. C'mon, we're leaving."

This is super short, but there's a 99,9% chance that I will update again today so bare with me!

Who do y'all think is gonna be responsible for this?

XO

LadyBug

Chapter 25

"I'm still not sure this is a good idea," I mumbled as Morgan drove around Nashville to find the address Seth had sent him.

"Yeah, well, it's been two hours and Seth still hasn't called me back so, I'm not gonna just wait around."

"I don't want you to get yourself in trouble, that's all," I added softly.

"I will get in trouble if I need to, I don't care what anyone has to say. Family comes first and I won't let something slide with Ellie that I wouldn't with Indie. It just don't work like that."

I had to admit that seeing him get so involved to protect my daughter was making me fall in love with him even more. I had been hiding the pregnancy from him because I thought that it might affect his reputation, but I now realized that Jared had been right all along. He didn't care about his reputation. Not when it came to his family. He loved Ellie more than her dad ever had and he was willing to get in the line of fire for her. I looked down at my baby bump, rubbing it softly. *You're one lucky kid. That man will never let anyone harm you.*

"We're here," he said, pulling into the parking space of a small building.

"Do we know the apartment number?" I asked.

"We do, it's- Wait," he said, squinting his eyes. His face changed when the realization hit him. "That's Katie's car."

"Are you sure? It could just be the same-"

"That stupid fucking bumped sticker?" he said, pointing to a sticker that read Badass Cowgirl. "Yeah, I'm sure."

"You really think she would go that far? To post pictures of Ellie online? Just to get back at me?" I said, not wanting to believe a mom would actually do that to a fellow mom.

"Well, we're here, aren't we, Aubrey?" He snapped.

"That's fucked up."

He jumped out of his truck and I ran after him.

"Do you even know whose apartment this is?" I asked, while he rang the doorbell aggressively. He shook his head no.

"Who's this?" A man's voice asked over the intercom.

"Morgan. Open up," he ordered sternly. There was a short silence and a woman's voice took over.

"Why are you here? Are you following me?" Katie said.

"Open that fucking door before I break it down, Katie."

"Morgan," I warned him softly. He kept ringing the doorbell when we finally heard a buzzing sound and a soft click letting us know that the door was unlocked. Morgan rushed up the stairs and I followed him. He knocked on the door of apartment number 8 and a guy -pretty good looking guy, if I'm being honest- opened the door.

"Yeah?" He asked.

"Where the fuck is she?" Morgan asked, obviously agitated.

"Daddy!!" I heard a little voice yell from inside the apartment. A tiny hand grabbed the door and opened it slightly wider and Indie poked his head out, beaming at his dad.

"Hi, buddy," Morgan said softly, picking him up. "Where's mama?"

"In the kitchen," he said, placing a cute peck on Morgan's cheek.

"Can you get Katie, man?" Morgan told the guy impatiently.

"Sure, sorry bro. I'm Luke, by the way. I know we met at the hospital, but I didn't really get to introduce myself. I really like your music man, I-"

"Luke!" Katie said angrily, forcing him to shut up. He got out of her way and she came to face us.

"Why are you here, Morgan," she asked dryly. "Why are you both here, actually?"

"Where the fuck do you get off?!" Morgan said. I saw Indie's expression change and a concerned look took over his little face.

"Hey, Indie! Remember me?" I asked, trying to distract him. He nodded shyly. "Do you want to go for a walk? I saw a cute ice cream place around the corner-"

"He's not going anywhere," Katie snapped, taking him from Morgan's arms and putting him down inside the apartment. "Go play," she told him. I sighed.

"I know it was you, Seth tracked the IP address of that post. Reddit, Katie? Really?" Morgan said.

"What the fuck are you even going on about? Are you drunk, boy?"

"Why would you do that?" I asked. "You want to hate me? That's fine. You want to expose me online or make me look like just another brainless groupie he's messing around with? Also fine, I'm a big girl, I can handle it. But why did you have to bring my child into this? That's messed up. I would have never done something like that to you, or your son," I said calmly, trying to stay level-headed.

"I didn't take the pictures," she said.

"I don't doubt that," I responded. "But, you still posted them. Why?"

"Why not? You wanna play super dad for the cameras with that baby on your hip, but you can't take a little bit of heat?" She chuckled dryly, looking at Morgan.

"It's not about me you fucking psycho!" he yelled at her.

"Hey, your kid is here, keep it down," I whispered, trying to get him to calm down, at least for Indie's sake. He sighed.

"See, this? Right here?" He said pointing at me. "What she just told me? That is a prime example of why she'll never stoop as low as you. Hurting a kid to get to me, Katie? That kind of shit is exacly why, even with Indie in the mix, I never even thought of getting back together with you," he snapped. "Take that shit down or god help me I will sue the fuck out of you and suck you dry. And that kid in there that you just snapped at?" He said, pointing at Indie's little blond hair. "He's the one paying for all that cosmetic bullshit you ruined your face with. So maybe try being a decent fucking mom so I don't change my mind and sue you for full custody," he spat. I was speechless. I had never seen him so angry. Every word he spoke to her felt like a dagger coming out of his mouth. "I'm giving you one hour before I press charges."

She slammed the door in his face angrily and he grabbed me by the arm, dragging me down the stairs with him.

"Morgan," I said softly. He ignored me and kept pulling on my arm.

"Babe, you're hurting me!" I snapped, pulling my arm away from him.

"Sorry," he mumbled. "I'm just so fucking pissed. Of all people, she had to be one who done this. I fucking hate her. I pity that poor goof who-"

"Morgan," I stopped him. "You didn't tell Indie goodbye." He sighed and looked at me.

"How is your heart always in the right place like that? How do you do it?" he asked. I shrugged. "We'll come pick him up tomorrow after the house showings. It's my week anyway."

"So, do we have to sleep here tonight?" I asked nervously. He looked at his watch.

"We don't have to but, it is getting late and we do have an early morning," he shrugged.

"If I agree to this, am I gonna find someone else's shit in your house?" I asked, biting my fingernails. He chuckled.

"No one else's stuff. Just the stuff you left in my dressing room in Milwaukee."

"You kept it?" I asked, genuinely shocked.

"Yeah," he admitted, embarrassed. "I held out hope."

"Alright then," I finally gave in.

"Look at you, learning to trust me," he joked. I rolled my eyes and he placed a gentle kiss on the top of my head. If I wasn't convinced before of the lengths this man would go to for Ellie and I, I definitely was now.

Alright so, I have an insanely high fever right now and I'm heavily medicated so if this absolutely sucks please let me know and I'll delete it and try again when I feel better lmao

Also, we made it to 1.5k views! Thanks to each and every one of you!

XO

LadyBug

Chapter 26

A couple of weeks had passed since the airport incident. Katie had taken down her post a mere 15 minutes after Morgan and I had left her boyfriend's place. A few news outlets had still made articles on the subject and shared some of the pictures but all of them had had the common sense of blurring Ellie's face, which, honestly, was all I had wanted in the first place. Indie had spent two of the last four weeks with us, which had given us time to bond as a family. Both kids were excited to know that they would become older siblings and were already trying to get as involved as possible in their new roles.

Morgan and I were in escrow on a gorgeous 5 bedroom single family home on Acklen Avenue in Nashville. The house was modern, somewhat like the one he already had (which was now for sale), but still felt like a home that you could comfortably raise children in, with a nice yard and a park right around the corner. Ellie, Indie and the new baby would all get their own room which they were very excited about.

Morgan had been booked to play tonight at this local festival in Nashville. After over a month of being home and not getting to perform for anyone other than the kids and I, it was safe to say he was very excited to be playing in front of a crowd again. Ellie and I would be coming out to see him and it was going to be her very first concert. Katie and her boyfriend Luke had also asked Morgan for tickets so that they could bring Indie along, which I have to admit I was far from stoked about.

"Your mom's coming with us," I told Morgan. "We don't need to have her and her boyfriend hanging around, we can bring Indie by ourselves."

"I know, baby," he said, taking my hands into his. "And I totally understand why you don't want to see her, but it's her week with him. I already offered that we take him but she doesn't want to. I don't want to penalize my son over his mom's behavior. It would be shitty to make him miss out on something just 'cause we don't want her around. Don't you think?" He asked softly, looking into my eyes.

"You're right," I admitted.

"Imagine if my next baby mama don't like you, I can't penalize the baby for that!"

"Boy, I swear to God, if you-"

"I'm kidding," he laughed.

"Not funny," I snapped, giving him side eye.

"You're stuck with me," he said, pulling me into his chest and kissing the top of my head. "After all I've had to go through to get you to actually go out with me, there's no way I'm letting you go."

I secretly smiled against his shirt. I had to admit I don't think I had ever loved anyone the way I loved him. I had never been able to trust Josh, and with good reason. But, even though it had taken time for me to be able to fully trust Morgan, I could now confidently say that I couldn't imagine my life without him, nor did I want to.

We got to the venue a couple of hours before the show. People didn't only recognize Morgan; they were starting to recognize me too. I knew this would happen sooner or later; the amount of instagram followers I had had increased insanely since we had started dating publicly, but I still wasn't sure how to feel about it. People recognized Katie too, which I guess felt kind of bittersweet. I knew no matter what I did, she'd always be the mother of his eldest kid and I would have to figure out a way to put my personal feelings aside. But seeing how comfortable she was being recognized felt weird.

Morgan got on stage at 8:30 and the energy emitting from the crowd was breathtaking. Ellie was so excited to watch him play, I had to keep her from running on stage with him a few times. Lesli had dressed her up in Morgan's merch from head to toe and was proudly carrying her around on her hip.

"Are you Aubrey?" a teenage girl asked, making me turn around to face her.

"I am," I told the stranger. "Do we know each other?" I asked. She shook her head no.

"My dad works for the festival. I am a huge fan of Morgan's. Can we take a picture?" she asked timidly.

"You want to take a picture with me?" I asked, confused.

"Yeah, it'll look good for the 'gram," she giggled.

"Oh, um, sure," I said awkwardly.

"I'll take it for you," Katie said, grabbing the phone out of the girl's hands. Great. I smiled awkwardly, posing for the picture. The girl took her phone back and looked at the photo.

"Awesome, thanks!" she said before leaving the backstage area. I smiled at her, still not sure of why she wanted me to be in her picture.

"You'll get used to it," Katie told me, smiling faintly.

"Oh, I don't know about that," I sighed, returning the faint smile. She walked closer to me.

"You can't avoid it so, might as well roll with the punches," she giggled.

"I guess so," I shrugged.

"I know you hate me," she sighed.

"I don't hate you," I admitted. "I don't particularly like you, but I don't hate you."

"Then you're a better person than most people 'cause you would have every reason to," she chuckled dryly.

"I love your son," I said. "He's a sweet kid and I want him to be comfortable around me. And if that means I have to bite my tongue and put my personal feelings aside then so be it."

"You're a good person," she said, seemingly genuine. "And I know you've been nice to Indie. He's told me all about it."

"I try to be," I shrugged.

"I'm sorry for the pictures. You were right, I shouldn't have involved your daughter in this. I'm sorry."

"It's okay, we all make mistakes. I shouldn't have said what I said to you when Indie was in the hospital," I admitted.

"He's never introduced our son to another woman before you," she confessed, looking at

Morgan. "I guess it just stung to know my baby would be around another girl. Still doesn't excuse what I did, but I didn't know how to act if I'm being honest."

I had never even thought of that. Because Josh had never taken care of Ellie, I guess that had never been part of my concerns. But, seeing my daughter around another woman would have definitely made me feel some type of way. I could easily relate to that.

"Well, if ever you want to get to know me, outside of the crazy drama that has been going on between us, you can just call me, you know? We could grab coffee or something," I suggested. She smiled.

"I would love that."

Morgan's set was coming to an end and the kids were both falling asleep in their strollers. He was playing his last song of the night and the crowd was singing along every single word. I smiled, looking at him. He was so passionate about his music. I felt like I could watch him play for hours on end. I'm so fucking in love with you, Morgan wallen.

"Well, well, well. If this isn't my little Aubrey, all grown up," a voice said from behind me, pulling me out of my thoughts. I turned around to see who it was and immediately felt my blood run cold.

"Mom?"

Let me know what you guys think!

Xo

LadyBug

Chapter 27

"Mom?" I asked. This couldn't be real, I had to be imagining things. I felt as though I had just seen a ghost.

"Well, don't I get a hug?" She smiled, opening her arms.

"Why are you here?" I asked dryly.

"Do you need me to get security?" Katie whispered. I shook my head no.

"I came to see my favorite daughter. And where is this granddaughter of mine? I ought to meet her!" She said, looking for Ellie left and right.

"Why are you here, mom?!" I snapped. "I haven't seen you in over five years. You've never even asked to see my daughter. So, why are you here now?!"

Morgan thanked the crowd and got off the stage, running towards me and pulling me in for a hug.

"Did you like it? Did Ellie like it?" He asked, placing a soft kiss on my lips.

"You must be Morgan," she stated, interrupting our kiss. "I'm Stevie," she said, pulling her hand out to shake his. Morgan looked at me confused. "Aubrey Jean's mom."

Morgan shook her hand, still confused.

"No one calls me Aubrey Jean anymore."

"Well, when you push a kid out of your vagina, you get to call her whatever you like, don't you?" She said, laughing by herself. I rolled my eyes.

"You didn't tell me your mom was coming," Morgan said, laughing awkwardly.

"Oh, that's because Stevie didn't tell anyone she was coming," I answered, smiling at him while my eyes were screaming help me. Morgan looked around uncomfortably.

"How did she even make it past security?" he whispered into my ear. I shrugged.

"I was a groupie in the 80s, spent my teens and early twenties following bands around. I know all the tricks," she said, winking at him. I sighed, seriously embarrassed by her behavior. "So, I read online that you got my daughter pregnant," she told Morgan.

"Mom, why are you even-"

"You oughta get her a ring too," she told him. My jaw dropped to the floor. "Take it from me, son. No woman wants two babies from two different men and not one ring."

"And no woman wants her absent mother to show up unannounced, yet here you are," I snapped.

"Always so feisty, Aubrey Jean. I wonder how you could even get a man like him to have a baby with you with that mouth of yours."

"Don't speak to her like that," Morgan intervened calmly.

"Oh, boy. You still have a lot to learn about my daughter. Trust me, once she's done playing with you she'll toss you to the side just like she did me."

"Cry me a fucking river," I mumbled.

"What a girl wouldn't do for money and fame," she added.

"A girl like you, maybe," I snapped.

"So, little girl or little boy this time?" she asked, putting her hands on my belly. I took a step back.

"We don't know yet," Morgan said. "We're finding out tomorrow."

"Well, isn't this exciting! Either way, that little shrimp in there got you settled for life," she laughed, winking at me. I stared at her, my gaze filled with disgust, too shocked to even say anything back.

"We should go," I told Morgan. "Your mom's already waiting in the car with El and I'm pretty sure Indie left-"

"Before you go, don't you have a few bucks for your mama? I don't even know where I'm gonna sleep tonight. Or, I could come home with you, help take care of y-"

"Absolutely fucking not," I stopped her. "And we don't have any money to give to you."

"Really, Aubrey Jean? After all I have done for you, not even a few bucks to spare?"

Morgan waved at Seth, asking him to come see us.

"Good show, man. The fans seemed pretty happy and-" Seth babbled before Morgan cut him off.

"Get her a hotel room for tonight, put it on my card," he told him, pointing to Stevie.

"Babe, you don't have to-" I started.

"It's alright," he said softly, kissing the top of my head. "It was nice meeting you, Stevie. Have a good night," he smiled faintly before grabbing my hand and turning around. We walked towards the exit, followed by security, and made our way to the car where Lesli and Ellie were waiting for us. Ellie had already fallen asleep in her car seat by the time we got there.

"What took you two so long," Lesli asked. "Actually, I don't wanna know-"

"Nothing like that," I assured her. "My mom showed up."

"Oh," she said. "And, is that good news or bad news?"

"Bad news. Very bad news. And you should not have put her into a hotel room," I told Morgan dryly.

"What was I supposed to do? Leave her out on the street?"

"She never took care of me, why should we take care of her?!" I snapped.

"Alright, calm down, Aubrey Jean," he chuckled.

"Do not fucking call me that. God, you can be such a dick sometimes, I-"

"I'm kidding," he said softly, taking my hand into his. I pulled it away instantly.

"You have no idea what it's like to be forced to live with a parent who doesn't care about you! I was six years old the first time that woman left me alone, Morgan! That's three years older than Ellie. She left me alone for two weeks with no food and no money. I had to fend for myself at six years old and that was only the first of many times."

"You poor thing," Lesli said softly.

"And she'll never leave!" I continued. "They're gonna charge your credit card until the day she dies because good luck getting her out of that freaking hotel room you put her in."

"It's not like that's what's gonna put us on the street," he said calmly.

"That's not the point! She doesn't get to just come back and mooch off of us, not after everything she's done to me. I don't want to do shit for her!"

"It's fine, you're not. I am!"

"Seriously?" I asked, baffled by his comment.

"Morgan," his mom warned.

"I don't mean it like that. Just, like, you don't want to do anything for her and I get that but you don't have to worry about that, it's not you-"

"Boy, shut your damn mouth!" His mom snapped.

"I thought what's mine is yours and what's yours is mine, but I guess we're past that now." I snapped.

"That's not- Just cancel the damn credit card, they'll throw her out, I don't care. I don't wanna fight with you!" He argued.

"Do whatever you want, Morgan. Not my money," I said, looking out the window. I heard him sigh but refused to look at him.

"Aubrey," he said while I ignored him. "Aubrey!"

"What?" I asked dryly, not taking my eyes off the window.

"Look at me," he said softly. "Please."

"I don't even wanna see your face right now."

Chapter 28

We pulled into Lesli's driveway and I jumped out immediately. I went around the car and got Ellie out of her car seat.

"Let me help you," Morgan said.

"I've been doing it by myself for three years, I don't need your help," I snapped. I grabbed Ellie and started carrying her towards the house with Morgan following me.

"I know you can do it by yourself, but you shouldn't be doing heavy lifting. Jared said-"

"Morgan, I need you to get the fuck off my case right now," I snarled. He sighed. I tried to go up the front porch but missed the first step and fell on my side. Ellie woke up and started crying instantly.

"Fuck," I whispered, feeling a sharp pain in my lower abdomen.

"Baby, are you okay?" Morgan asked, genuinely concerned.

"I'm alright. Can you take Ellie to bed?"

"I'll take her," Leslie said, picking her up softly and carrying her in. I felt tears well up in my eyes and Morgan noticed right away.

"Are you hurt, Aubrey? Don't act tough, tell me if you are it's import-"

"I think my water broke," I breathed, pointing at the wet spot in my jeans.

"Shit," Morgan said. "Can you walk?" He asked, getting me up off the ground. I nodded. "Alright, I'm taking you to the hospital."

He held my thigh throughout the drive while I tried to hide the tears that were running down my face. I was 20 weeks pregnant. Halfway through a full term pregnancy. I knew full well that if I gave birth right now, the chances of my baby surviving would be slim to none.

"I should have let you help me," I cried.

"You never listen to me," Morgan said dryly. "Every time I try to help it fucking backfires. It's like you don't even know me well enough to understand that I always have good intentions when it comes to you."

He was right. I was guarded, and I'd always been guarded by fear of getting hurt, or betrayed. And now, I had put our baby in jeopardy because I was too hard headed to admit I needed help. I wanted to avoid showing weakness so bad that I had gotten my priorities all wrong.

"I'm sorry," I whispered, my voice breaking.

"It was reckless," he stated dryly.

"Morgan, I said I was sorry. I can't go back in time. What do you want me to do?" I cried softly. He didn't answer.

He pulled into the ER's parking lot and came to open the door for me and helped me climb out of his truck. I wiped my tears quickly and he helped me walk to the triage desk. The nurse gave us forms to fill out and said that a doctor would be calling us shortly and that I should let my practitioner know that I'd be getting admitted, so Morgan took it upon himself to call Jared.

"Hey man, sorry, I know it's late, but we're in the hospital," Morgan told Jared. I couldn't hear what he was saying. "Yeah, she fell in the stairs with Ellie in her arms, she says she thinks her water broke," he stated. His face changed all of a sudden. "I know that, Jared. She insisted, wouldn't let me take her-" "No," he continued. "You know how she gets when things don't go her way!" He defended himself. I started at him.

"I'm right here," I said.

"Ms. Aubrey Farrell, room 5," someone called over the intercom.

"We gotta go Jared, they're calling us," he said before hanging up. He helped me up and we walked into the room where the doctor was already waiting for us.

"Hi, Ms. Farrell. I am Dr. Chris Engler. I read on your chart that you have lost some amniotic fluid, would you mind telling me what happened?"

"She fell down the stairs with a three year old in her arms, that I should've been carrying but-"

"I fell," I mumbled, cutting him off.

"Okay, I see you haven't had the anatomy scan, you were scheduled to have it tomorrow, so we will do a quick ultrasound and we'll do that as well while we're here," he smiled.

"Okay," I mumbled nervously. Dr. Engler gave me a little nod and walked out the room to go get the ultrasound machine.

"I'm nervous," I confessed, laying down on the bed. Morgan took my hand and kissed it gently.

"I'm nervous too. I'm sorry for snapping at you earlier, I know you didn't do it on purpose. I just feel like you don't really want me around sometimes," he admitted.

"Morgan, what?" I asked, shocked by his comment. I looked into his eyes. "You're the only person I've ever wanted around Ellie-"

"Yeah, I know you want me around Ellie, but sometimes I feel like you don't want me around you. Like, you keep me around just 'cause I'm good for Ellie and the baby."

"Do you really feel that way?" I asked, feeling deeply saddened by what he had just shared with me.

"Listen, I know we haven't had the most conventional beginning, and I know I've hurt you, along with a lot of people in your life, and that you have a hard time letting go of things sometimes. But, you don't ever hold my hand, or kiss me, or show in any damn way that you even like me. I do those things because I'm ridiculously in love with you but I often find myself thinking that this might be a one way street. I think you like the way I treat you and Ellie. I think you like my family and you feel kinda safe around me, but do you even love me, Aubrey?"

Dr. Engler walked back in, rolling in the ultrasound machine and putting an end to our conversation at the worst possible time. Part of me was happy to see him walk back in because I was genuinely terrified that something might have happened to my baby, but the other part needed to let Morgan know how much I loved him and how much he meant to me. Right now. I can't believe he feels that way. I'm no better to him than Josh was to me.

"Alright, Ms. Farrell. I'm gonna need you to lift up your shirt," he said calmly, getting the equipment set up. I did as told quietly, trying to avoid Morgan's eyes. "Great, this might feel a little cold," he said, squirting the blue gel onto my stomach and sliding the probe on it. The sound of the baby's heartbeat filled the room almost instantly. I sighed in relief and Morgan grabbed my hand.

"That's your baby's heartbeat. Nice and strong," Dr. Engler said. Morgan looked at me and I could see the tears of joy shining in his gorgeous blue eyes. He kissed my hand softly.

"Our baby's heartbeat," he whispered, not taking his eyes off me. I smiled at him.

"I love you," I mouthed quietly. He smiled and wiped his tears off quickly.

"There's the head," Dr. Engler said, pointing towards the screen. I smiled. God is great.

"Everything seems to be fine, Ms. Farrell. Your baby is healthy and growing. Losing a little amniotic fluid can happen, and while not alarming, it does mean that you're going to have to be extra careful. No heavy lifting, as little stress as possible and lots and lots of resting. Your partner seems to be willing and involved; let him help. You might not want to admit it, but you need the help. Okay?" He asked, looking at me. I nodded.

"I like him," Morgan said, pointing to Dr. Engler. "Listen to him, let me help. Please," he said softly. Dr. Engler chuckled.

"Okay," I nodded, smiling faintly.

"Do you want to know the sex of the baby?" Dr. Engler asked. Morgan and I exchanged a look and both nodded.

"Yes," I confirmed.

"Congratulations, you're having a little girl."

Hemingway said "write drunk, edit sober" and while I love the write drunk part, the sober editing gets kind of boring at times lmao

I usually just quickly proof read the chapters right before I post them. Now, I think I might turn this into a series (2 or 3 books) and take a week or two between each books to just go back and edit stuff. All this to say, I'm sorry about the terrible grammar and syntax! I promise I will fix it all in a couple weeks!

I hope y'all like this! While the last few chapters have been getting more views, they've also been getting less votes and comments so, fingers crossed that the readers that have been here since the beginning still like the story now!

XO LadyBug

Chapter 29

"Congratulations, you're having a little girl."

I turned to look at Morgan who was wiping happy tears off his face. He chuckled.

"I'm gonna have a daughter," he whispered.

"You're gonna have a daughter," I whispered back to him, smiling.

"I will leave you guys some privacy. You're free to go. Ms. Farrell, make sure to let your practitioner know that you were in today. If you don't have one, this is my card," he said, handing me his business card. "You can call my secretary and I will take you on as a patient. Have a good night," he smiled, shaking Morgan's hand quickly before exiting the room.

"Thank god she's okay," I mumbled, looking at my baby bump.

"Please, tell me you've learned your lesson," he said softly. "Don't let your pride get in the way of things. Especially not with me, please," he begged. I nodded.

"You're right," I admitted. "And, I know you didn't put my mom into a hotel room to piss me off. I overreacted, you didn't know and-"

Our lips touched, putting an end to my rambling. Soft lips on soft lips, finding their match in warmth. I could smell the forest mint of his shampoo flirting with my nostrils. He hadn't kissed me like this in a couple of weeks. A kiss that made me feel like the only girl he'd ever truly loved. The kind of kiss that screamed infatuation and that made my heart beat a little bit faster. I felt his hands touch my face, cupping my cheeks ever so gently and softly pulling me in closer. His lips parted slightly, allowing my tongue to slip inside and his hands quickly ran from my cheeks to my breasts, in the heat of the moment. He panted into my mouth, touching me gently and making me shiver in anticipation. He let his left hand trail to the back of my bra, trying to unhook it when the door swung wide open. We both jumped, pulling away from one another.

"Sorry," a nurse mumbled, closing the door as soon as she witnessed the scene. I looked at Morgan, absolutely mortified and he bursted out laughing.

"Stop laughing," I giggled. "That's so embarrassing."

"We're fine," he laughed. "C'mon, we can stop for food on the way home," he said, grabbing my hand and helping me off the hospital bed.

"You really know the way to a pregnant woman's heart," giggled, walking out of the room, holding his hand in mine.

We made our way to the car and he opened the door for me. I sat down and looked at him, still standing outside next to me.

"Come here," I said, gesturing to him to come closer with my index finger. He took a step forward, leaving only a few inches between us.

"I love you so much, Morgan. Knowing that you don't feel it genuinely breaks my heart, but you have to believe me. I love you more than words can even describe," I whispered, looking deep into his eyes. He smiled.

"I love you too," he said, placing a soft kiss on my lips before walking around the truck to go sit in the driver's seat.

***

We got home a couple of hours later after having stopped for food along the way and driven around in circles, debating how we should name our daughter. Lesli was sitting on the front porch, waiting for us. Morgan helped me get out of the truck and held my hand as we walked up the steps.

"Careful this time," he joked.

"You're so funny," I giggled, rolling my eyes at him.

"Glad to see you two made up," Lesli said softly. "How are you, honey?"

"I'm fine. So is the baby," I smiled, rubbing my baby bump softly. Morgan stood behind me and wrapped his arms around my body, placing his hands over mine one my bump.

"Do you wanna know?" He asked Lesli.

"Know what?" She asked, confused.

"Take a guess, boy or girl?" I said, smiling at her.

"Oh, you guys found out?!" She asked, visibly excited. I nodded. "Lord, I don't know. Enough of these games, just tell me!" She requested, laughing.

"It's a little girl," Morgan said softly.

"You're gonna have a little girl?" she asked him softly, her voice breaking. Morgan nodded. "Oh, honey. You're gonna be the best dad a little girl could ask for," she said, getting up off her chair and taking him into her arms. "And you, my darling. Two little girls is such a blessing. We're gonna throw you the best baby shower," she smiled, excited.

"Oh, you don't have to-"

"Nonsense! His sisters will help me plan it, you won't have to lift a finger. This'll be your special day. Just a little something to welcome us into our family," she said, pulling me into her arms. I smiled. I felt my phone vibrate into the back pocket of my jeans. I pulled away from the hug and grabbed it to check who it was.

JARED, 1:46 AM

I'm getting on the plane in 10 minutes. I'll be in Sneedville in the morning. Hope you're okay xx

I showed Morgan the text and he looked at me.

"Seems unnecessary," he said dryly.

"What should I tell him?" I asked.

"I don't know, don't you think it's a bit intense that he jumps on a plane the minute he thinks you might not be okay? Without even asking us?"

"Maybe," I admitted. "But he's always been that way. He's protective of me, like a big brother," I assured him. He chuckled.

"Yeah, I can guarantee you I've never talked about my sisters the way he talked about you before we met."

"How did he talk about me?" I asked, confused. He looked at Lesli and back at me.

"It's getting late, we should go to bed," he said softly.

"Alright, goodnight, kids," she smiled. Morgan walked into the house and I followed him. We got into our room quietly so as to not wake Ellie and closed the door.

"How did Jared speak of me before we met, Morgan?" I asked, again.

"He's in love with you!"

"He's told you that? Explicitly?" I asked, not sure whether to believe him or not.

"He's told me things that have led me to understand that he's in love with you. That's why I tried not to get involved with you at first."

"Didn't really try that hard," I joked. He rolled his eyes.

"Has it never crossed your mind that maybe he kept your pregnancy a secret 'cause he wanted to play the hero? Be that guy who, like, marries you and helps you raise your kid to save your honor."

"This isn't the 18th century. I don't need to be saved, my honor's fine," I laughed.

"That's not- My point is; it didn't cross your mind that he wanted to raise the baby with you? That by not telling me he was basically getting me out of the picture?"

"He wanted me to tell you! He even threatened to tell you himself if I didn't," I said.

"Yeah, well, he didn't tell me shit."

"I think you're making a mountain out of a molehill," I said, putting my hand on his shoulder gently. He sighed.

"If you say so," he gave in. "But, we're moving into the new house in a week and he does not get to move in with us. He has plenty of family in Sneedville, his parents are here, he does not need-"

"I promise, I won't ask him to come live with us," I giggled.

"It's our house. For us. And our kids. That's it. No one else, like you wanted," he said softly. I smiled.

"I know baby, just us."

Thanks to everyone for the extra love y'all sent me last night! Every comment/vote goes straight to my heart. I'm glad to know people are still engaging with this!

XO

LadyBug

Chapter 30

"Jared's here," Morgan said, waking me up. I opened my eyes and stretched slowly.

"What time is it?" I asked

"8:15 AM" he said dryly. I yawned.

"Why is he here so early?" I asked, rubbing my eyes softly. Morgan shrugged.

"To save the princess, I guess," he said, obviously bitter that Jared was even here to begin with. I rolled my eyes.

"Come here," I requested, pulling him onto the bed with me. "Just five more minutes," I begged, resting my head onto his chest and snuggling up against his warm body. He kissed the top of my head.

"C'mon, I'll make you some fresh juice," he said, gently getting me off of him and hopping out of bed.

"Juice? It's 8 o'clock in the morning, sir. I want coffee," I giggled.

"No more coffee."

"Why?"

"Because, Dr. Engler said to be extra careful," he said softly, putting a strand of hair behind my ear.

"Yeah, about heavy lifting and stuff, not about coffee!" I frowned.

"Baby-"

I got out of bed instantly, threw on one of Morgan's oversized shirts and ran out of the bedroom.

"Jaaared??" I yelled from the hallway.

"Yeah?"

"Can I have coffee?" I asked, sitting down on the couch next to him. Morgan came and stood behind me.

"Dr. Engler said to be careful, Aubrey. I just want what's good-"

"She can safely have 200mg per day, which is roughly two regular sized cups of coffee. No more than that though," he said, cutting Morgan off. I smiled.

"See?" I told Morgan. "I told you I could have some."

"Do whatever you want, Aubrey," he sighed. "I think I'm gonna go fishing."

"Babe, I didn't mean to-"

"It's fine," he said. "I just need to clear my head, that's all."

"Stress is worse than coffee for the baby, if you want my opinion," Jared mumbled.

"Not that I particularly want your opinion, but what exactly is that supposed to mean?" Morgan asked arrogantly.

"Guys, it's not-" I started before Jared cut me off.

"Fighting with your pregnant girlfriend -who should be your pregnant wife, if you ask me- is not only dumb and immature, but it's also bad for your child."

"Are you calling me immature? 'Cause, I don't know, but it seems to me that someone hiding a pregnancy from the baby's dad, who's supposed to be your best friend, by the way, is kinda-"

"You both are fucking stressing me out right now!" I snapped. "What the fuck is this? Are y'all trying to figure out who has the biggest swinging dick?!"

"I'd win that for sure," Morgan chuckled.

"It doesn't mean what you think it means, idiot," Jared added.

"Seriously, guys?! How old are you?!" I said, getting seriously annoyed by them both.

"Can I go fishing now or will that stress you out too much, mama?" Morgan asked. I rolled my eyes.

"Go, I'm fine," I sighed, rubbing my forehead. He kissed the top of my head gently.

"I'll be back in a few hours. Call if you need anything," he said softly, slowly turning back into the person I knew and loved. "I love you."

"I love you too," I said, watching him leave.

"Is he always like that?" Jared asked as soon as Morgan had closed the door.

"Are you?" I snapped, letting him know I didn't think he was innocent in this.

"I'm on your side!" He defended himself.

"There are no sides, Jared! He's my boyfriend and the father of my kid!"

"Still no ring though." he shrugged.

"Why are you acting like that?" I asked, shocked by his comment. "I don't even recognize you right now."

"Because, I've thought about it and it was wrong of me to try and force you into telling him about the baby. You deserve someone who's 100 percent in!"

"He is 100 percent in! He's buying me a house and we-"

"Buying you a house don't mean shit to him. It won't even make a dent in his bank account. You can't measure commitment with material things when you're dating someone like that. Where's the ring, Aubrey?"

"I didn't want the ring!" I snapped. He looked into my eyes softly.

"Really?" he mumbled.

"Yeah, I wasn't ready to-" Jared put a strand of my hair behind my ear and got closer to me. "What are you doing?" I asked.

"For a minute, I really thought you were gonna marry him, but knowing you said no," he said, cupping my left cheek in his hand and getting his face closer to mine. The door opened abruptly and Morgan walked in.

"What the fuck," he whispered, staring at Jared who still had his hand on my face. I slapped his arm lightly to get him off me.

"Baby, it's not-" I started.

"Get the fuck out of here," Morgan told Jared dryly.

"Morgan, man, this isn't-"

"Are you out of your goddamn mind?! Making moves on my pregnant girlfriend?! Get the fuck out of here before I throw you out, Jared," he said, getting more and more agitated. Jared got off the couch.

"I came all the way from Vermont to make sure she was okay and this is how you're gonna treat me?!"

"No one fucking asked you to come, man! There are other doctors, alright?! Now get the fuck out of my house," he yelled. Jared looked at me.

"Really, Aubrey? That's fine with you?"

"I don't know, Jared. It's- I have to clear my head right now," I admitted. He chuckled dryly.

"Wow," he whispered before turning on his heels and heading out. Morgan slammed the door.

"I'm gonna give you a chance to explain because I know in my core that you're not that type of girl, but I have zero patience for bullshit right now, Aubrey, I'm warning you" he said, obviously heated. "What the fuck was that?"

"I don't know," I mumbled.

"Seriously?!"

"I swear, I don't know what happened! He was telling me how I deserve someone who's a 100% in and that you buying me a house didn't mean a thing because you have so much money and-"

"Wow, that is fucking rich coming from him."

"He told me, like, where's the ring? So I said I didn't want the ring cause I wasn't ready and-"

"You told him you didn't wanna marry me..?" He asked, visibly hurt.

"I just said I wasn't ready," I shrugged.

"Would've been nice of you to let me know that before you went and told Jared," he snapped.

"I did tell you. I told you when you asked me to marry you in my freaking kitchen in Vermont!"

"You told me you didn't want to marry me like that. Because, you didn't want to rush into things and that I wasn't making it romantic. You didn't tell me you didn't wanna marry me at all. That changes things."

"Why does that change things?" I asked confused.

"Because, I- Fuck!" he said angrily. "I just wish you would've fucking told me that, Aubrey. Now, what? He thinks it's fair game? Is he right?! Is that what you want?! Fucking, best man wins?!"

"No, I- You're overreacting! I never said I didn't want to marry you ever! I just said I didn't want to rush into things!"

"Rush into things?! You're fucking pregnant with my kid! What could you possibly be rushing into at this point?"

"I don't want you to want to marry me just because I'm pregnant!" I yelled. "I want you to want to marry me for me!"

"I do want to marry you for you! What the fuck did you tell Jared?"

"Weren't you supposed to go fishing?!" I said, trying to avoid the conversation as I felt my eyes well up with tears.

"I left my phone inside, my bad! Maybe I should've waited until he had bent you over on the couch!"

"Stop yelling at me!" I said, tears rolling down my cheeks. He sighed.

"Maybe I shouldn't sell my house just yet. Maybe you and Ellie should move into the new house and I should just wait. See if we can even make this work."

I hope you guys like this!

XO

LadyBug

Chapter 31

"Maybe I shouldn't sell my house just yet. Maybe you and Ellie should move into the new house and I should just wait. See if we can even make this work," Morgan said, his eyes fully detached from me.

I had given up on trying to stop the tears from flowing.

"Please, don't do this," I whispered, my voice breaking.

"If it's Ellie you're worried about, I can still take her on the same weeks I take Indie," he stated. While I was genuinely grateful to know he loved Ellie to the point where he was willing to continue being a father figure to her even if we weren't together, I didn't want to believe that he was actually suggesting that we spend time apart.

"It's not about Ellie," I cried. "I don't want to lose you."

"You're not losing me. I'm just saying that this clearly isn't working for you, and honestly Aubrey, being constantly in the line of fire isn't really working for me either. So, why don't we just spend some time separately to figure out if we're better apart than we are together."

"I don't want to be apart from you," I whispered. He looked at me and wiped my tears with his thumb. "I love you. I'm sorry if I didn't show it enough or if I did dumb shit. I'm sorry I didn't let you make me juice instead of coffee. I'm sorry I'm so fucking gated and hard headed all the time, I know I have work to do, but please don't do this."

"What if I hadn't walked in, Aubrey? Would you have kissed him? Slept with him, maybe?"

"No! God, No. I don't want Jared, Morgan. I want you," I cried softly.

"But you're not sure about me. You trust him a hell of a lot more than you trust me."

"I am sure about you!" I defended myself.

"Not enough to want to marry me," he mumbled, looking down. "The worst part is I was actually gonna ask you. I had this whole thing planned and- Doesn't matter," he said, stopping himself. "I asked him to help me pick the perfect ring for you and it's just- It's messed up. To think that you two were-," he sighed.

"Nothing happened between Jared and I. You have to believe me," I begged.

"I believe you, Aubrey. But had the situation been reversed, you wouldn't have believed me."

I hated to admit it but I knew deep down that he was probably right. Had I walked into a room where some girl was about to kiss him, I would probably have packed my bags right away. I could see where he was coming from, but I refused to let go. I wanted to be with him and I did love him. I loved him more than I'd ever loved anyone else. I felt like my brain was about to explode. I couldn't even fathom having to know he lived alone in that house while I was getting settled in the house he had bought for us and our growing family. The thought alone paralyzed me. All I could think of was how broken my heart felt, when I felt a kick in my stomach. I looked at Morgan, shocked.

"What?" He asked, confused. I took his hands and put them on my stomach. She kicked again.

"Did you feel that?" I asked. He smiled.

"Yeah, I felt it," he said, grinning, not taking his hands off me. She kicked again. "She's strong," he chuckled.

"She's telling you to stay," I mumbled. He grinned, avoiding my eyes, and kneeled in front of me, his hands still on my bump.

"Is that what's happening, babygirl?" He said softly, talking to my stomach. "You don't want me to be away from you and mama?" He asked, and the baby kicked again. "This is crazy," he said looking at me. "She's kicking so hard."

"I know," I said. "It hurts a little," I giggled, trying to wipe away the tears. "I think she likes the sound of your voice," I said softly. He looked into my eyes, got up off his knees and sat down next to me on the couch.

"I wish you loved me as much as I love you," he whispered, grazing my cheek softly with his thumb.

"Did you really get me a ring?" I asked, my voice breaking as I said the words out loud. He looked down and nodded slowly.

"It was dumb, it's jus-"

"Do you still want to marry me?" I whispered. He looked up to face me, his eyes locking in with mine. He nodded yes.

"Can I see it?" I asked.

"Like this, right now?"

"If you want, I mean you don't have to-"

"I want to," he said, cutting me off. "I had this whole thing planned where I was gonna take you out to the river and do this whole speech about how much you mean to me but, here," he said, pulling a box out of the backpocket of his jeans.

"You were planning on proposing today?" I asked, shocked. He nodded.

"That's why I wanted to go fishing," he said, using air quotes. "I wanted to pick the perfect spot and have a little set up ready for you with blankets and a couple of white Christmas lights hung up. Making it romantic, you know, like you wanted," he shrugged. I felt my eyes well up with tears.

"I'm so sorry," I whispered. "I ruined your plan. I would've loved that," I admitted.

"That's not what you told Jared," he mumbled.

"I didn't mean it like that. I meant that the reason we weren't engaged wasn't because of you, it was because of me. I was saying that to defend you," I mumbled.

"Girl, I don't need you to defend me. Especially not with Jared," he chuckled.

"I'm sorry. You're the most thoughtful and caring person I've ever met," I whispered.

"Do you wanna see the ring?" He asked. I nodded.

"Okay, let me do this properly," he said, getting on one knee in front of me. "Aubrey Jean F-"

"Just Aubrey," I whispered. He rolled his eyes. "I'm sorry, carry on," I mumbled.

"Jesus, woman," he chuckled. "Aubrey Farrell, no Jean, will you marry me?" he asked, opening the little jewelry box to show me the most beautiful yellow gold diamond ring I had ever seen. The band sparkled with marquise diamond vines throughout to perfectly compliment the center round-shaped diamond. It was breathtaking.

"That must have cost you a fortune," I whispered, covering my mouth with my right hand, not taking my eyes off the ring.

"Is that a yes?" he asked. I nodded frantically. He took my left hand gently and slid the ring on my finger. It was a perfect fit. I looked at my hand and back at Morgan.

"I love you so much," I whispered. He smiled.

"I love you too," he said, putting a strand of hair behind my ear and letting his soft lips dance one mine. I felt the butterflies in my stomach come alive. He pulled away softly.

"I got it engraved too," he said, pointing at the ring. I took it off and looked at the inscription inside.

"Forever yours, Morgan," I read out loud. "That's beautiful."

"Forever yours," he whispered to me.

"Forever yours."

Back at it again with some lovey dovey stuff! I hope y'all like that! What do you think should happen with Jared?

Xo

LadyBug

Chapter 32

A couple of weeks had passed since Morgan and I had gotten engaged. I was now 30 weeks pregnant and fully settled into our new Nashville home. Jared and I had not talked since the incident and my practitioner was now Dr. Engler. It pained me deeply to not have my best friend by my side through this huge milestone, but it felt, at times, like things could never go back to the way they were between us. Morgan had been adamant that he did not want me to see Jared by myself, and while I had absolutely no fear whatsoever that he would try to force himself onto me or anything like that, I still respected his wishes. I knew I'd probably be making similar requests, had I been in his shoes and so I did what I could to keep him as comfortable as possible with the situation. We hadn't set a date for our wedding yet, we had both agreed that we should wait until the baby was born and then play it by ear. We knew we'd be too busy as new parents to add planning a wedding to our list of responsibilities, so we decided to focus on our family for now. And I could genuinely say, for the first time in a long time, that I was happy. I had the man of my dreams taking care of me through every waking moment. My daughter had the best father figure I could have ever asked for and an amazing little brother whom she loved to play with. And I was going to have another baby that would be born in a house filled with love and joy, which is more than I could've dreamed of a year ago. The stars seemed to have finally aligned. I did miss Jared, I'd be lying if I said I didn't. But, I couldn't jeopardize my relationship with Morgan, even if it meant having to leave one of the most important people in my life behind. For now, at least.

Lesli and Morgan's sisters had planned an amazing baby shower for us. They had invited all of our friends and family to join us and celebrate our daughter.

"We have to pick a name, people are gonna ask us," Morgan said as we drove to Lesli's house for the party.

"You don't like any of the names I suggested!" I complained.

"Because, I don't want my daughter to end up with a name like Eleanor," he joked.

"Hey!" I said defensively. "Eleanor's a beautiful name, and you already have a step-daughter named Eleanor so that can't even happen," I frowned. He giggled, putting his hand on my thigh gently.

"I just want her to have a cool name, like Indie," he said.

"Ellie's a cool name! It was my grandma's name," I pouted.

"I know, I know," he said softly. "What about Willow?" He suggested. I snorted.

"Willow Wallen? Seriously? Willy Wonka while you're at it?" I laughed.

"I hadn't put both names together," he mumbled, rolling his eyes. "What about, Sailor?" He asked. I played with it in my head a little. Sailor Wallen. Definitely out of the box.

"I don't hate it," I said. He smiled.

"What about her middle name?" He asked.

"Lesli," I responded instantly.

"Really? You want to name her after my mom?" He confirmed softly, visibly touched by my answer. I nodded. "She'll be over the moon."

"So is that it? Did we just pick a name?" I asked him, excited. He chuckled.

"I think so. Sailor Lesli Wallen. It has a nice ring to it."

"It does," I agreed as he pulled into the driveway to his parents' house. Lesli was waiting for us on the porch, as per usual. I waved at her and she waved back. Morgan parked and came to help me climb out of his lifted truck.

"Aren't you a sight to see!" Lesli yelled as I walked towards her. "That little girl is really growing!" She said, pointing to my belly. I giggled.

"Yeah, a little too big if you ask me," I joked.

"Oh stop it, you're glowing," she said. "Everything's already set up. The girls have been working all morning. Most guests have arrived, we're just missing Jared and your uncle John," she told Morgan.

"You invited Jared?" He asked, shocked.

"Should I have not?" She responded, confused. "I mean he's your oldest friend and her best friend, no one told me not to-"

"It's fine, Lesli," I smiled. "Thank you for hosting such an amazing party for our little girl," I said, rubbing my bump softly and looking at Morgan, trying to get him to smile.

"Yeah, mom. Everything looks great," he mumbled, clearly lost in his thoughts. We made our way to the backyard area where the party was to be held.

"He might not even come," I assured him. He scoffed.

"As if he'd miss out on an opportunity to see you." I rolled my eyes. Morgan grabbed my hand and kissed my cheek.

"Either way, you're mine," he whispered in my ear. I couldn't help but to smile. We walked into the backyard and everyone was already there, mingling with each other, eating and drinking. The party was beautiful; Lesli and the girls had really pulled all the stops. Ernest was there with his wife Delaney and their son, Ryman, who was already running around with Ellie and Indie. They had brought a couple friends that Morgan seemed to know and who all seemed nice. Morgan's whole family was there as well; aunts, uncles, cousins, nieces and nephews. The whole gang. I looked around, trying to find somebody I knew well enough to go talk to when someone poked my shoulder lightly. I turned around.

"Hey," Jared said awkwardly. I smiled. A real heartfelt smile. I knew things had been messy between us, but seeing his face made me genuinely happy.

"Hey," I said softly.

"Congratulations," he said, handing me a pink teddy bear. I grinned, putting the plush animal next to my face.

"So cute," I giggled.

"Uncle Jared!!" Ellie yelled, running up to him and hugging his leg. Morgan, who was now a few feet ahead of me, turned back around as soon as he heard Ellie yelling. He frowned.

"Got some nerves showing up here," he told Jared.

"Your mom invited me, I thought you knew. I can leave if you-"

"Stay," I said, taking his hand into mine. "I'm happy to see you," I smiled. Morgan looked at me, disapproving of what I had just said.

"Can we have a sidebar for a second?" Morgan asked me, pullin me away from Jared. I followed him a little bit further, where we stood out of earshot.

"What the fuck, Aubrey?"

"Look, I'm happy to see him. I don't know anyone else here. It's all your friends and your family," I defended myself.

"You know my family!"

"Some of your family," I corrected.

"Well, you know Ernest, and you've met his wife-"

"Once."

"What?"

"I've met his wife once, Morgan. I don't know these people. Having met someone and knowing someone are two wildly different things. I know Jared. I know his heart and, sure, he messed up, but haven't I? And haven't you? I want him around for this part of our journey. He's my friend and he's yours too," I explained. He sighed.

"Fine, he can stay, but no-"

"Hi, Morgan!" A tall blonde girl said, interrupting us. "Do you remember me? I'm Delaney's friend, Georgia," she smiled. A big smile with perfect white teeth.

"Sure," he mumbled. I looked at him, confused by his reaction. He looked like he had just seen a ghost. He wasn't the type of guy who mumbled words in front of pretty girls. He was usually so confident, this didn't feel right. Something was up.

"Delaney told me you were getting married! Couldn't have guessed that the last time I saw you," she giggled. He put his arm around my waist, pulling me in closer to him.

"Yeah, getting married to the love of my life," he said, smiling at me. "So, Delaney invited you?" He asked, confused.

"Yeah, your mom apparently told her she could bring her girlfriends. She said it would be good for your fiance to meet some nice girls since she wasn't from here, so she brought a couple girls. Obviously Del' doesn't know what happened bet-"

"That's cool," he said, cutting her off. "It was nice to see you, uh, Georgia was it?" he asked. She nodded, smiling at him. "Alright, take care," he smiled before walking away with my hand in his. We went and sat on a bench by the little pond. He exhaled slowly.

"What the fuck kind of party is this?" he whispered to himself. "First, Jared. Now, this."

"Who is she?" I asked, not sure I wanted to hear the answer.

"Just some girl, a friend of Delaney's," he said casually, scratching the back of his head. Then the realization hit me.

"She's the one with the lacey red underwear isn't she?"

I hope y'all like this! All the votes and comments I got in the recent few days really do melt my heart!

Xo

LadyBug

Chapter 33

"She's the one with the lacey red underwear isn't she?" I asked, trying to swallow back tears. He bit the inside of his cheek and didn't answer. I could see him looking at me from the corner of his eye. I took a deep breath, trying not to let this ruin my day.

"You know, it's one thing to know you've been with a lot of women before me, it's a whole 'nother thing to find their underwear on your kitchen counter. But to actually meet her, Morgan; to have her come talk to my future husband, right in front of me, at my baby shower. That's just more than I can handle right now," I breathed, holding back tears.

"I don't even know why the fuck she's here, Aubrey," he whispered, scratching the back of his head.

"You know, you talk shit about Jared all the time. Telling me you don't want him around me when you know damn well he's my best fucking friend. Well guess what? I didn't sleep with Jared. But then I can't even have a freaking baby shower without being surrounded by the hoes you fucked before me. Are you serious, Morgan? How the fuck is that shit fair?!" I spat, angrily, knowing full well that if I didn't let the anger come out, the tears would. And there was no way I would cry in front of him -or Mrs. Red Underwear- right now.

"It's not! I know it's not, but it's not like I planned this-"

"See, that's exactly what you said when I found the damn underwear in the first place. Oh it's not like I planned this. Well, here's the thing, Morgan; whether you planned this or not couldn't matter less. It still fucking stings all the same."

I got up off the bench and he grabbed my hand softly.

"Where are you going? Please don't leave now," he whispered.

"I'm not gonna freaking leave. I wouldn't do that to your mom. I'm just gonna go talk to someone who actually gives a shit," I snapped. He sighed.

I walked away from the pond and started looking for Jared when my phone rang. I picked it up immediately.

"Hello?"

"Hi, my love! I heard you're having your baby shower today! I'm so sorry I couldn't be here," Chelsea said. I sighed.

"Girl, I miss you."

"I miss you too, how's life in Tennessee?" She asked.

"You're catching me on a weird day," I admitted. "Ask me again tomorrow?" I chuckled softly.

"Trouble in paradise?"

"something like that. If I fly you out, will you come over sometime? Soon?"

"Sure, I would love that!"

"Okay, we'll figure out something then. Talk soon?" I asked.

"Talk soon, Brey," she said before hanging up. I sighed. Damn I miss my girlfriend. I walked around looking for Jared and finally found him sitting under a willow tree, by himself.

"Hey," I said. He looked up to see who was talking to him and smiled at me.

"Hey."

"Can I sit with you?" I asked, sitting down without giving him time to answer.

***

Jared and I had now been sitting together and talking for nearly three hours. The sun had come down and people had started to leave.

"You know what sucks the most?" I asked.

"What?" He answered. I knew he was drunk by now, and so was everyone else at the party. Everybody had been sipping on wine and whiskey since the early hours of the afternoon and I was pregnant, which meant totally sober. But even drunk Jared was better company than sober Georgia, so I stayed hidden under that tree with him.

"What sucks the most," I continued. "Is that I can't fucking avoid his past conquests. It's like no matter what I do, no matter where I go, there's just some girl, waiting around the corner to tell me my soon-to-be husband fucked her brains out not too long ago," I complained. He chuckled into his drink.

"You're exaggerating," he said, laughing.

"Hardly. And don't defend him!"

"I'm not," he said, waving his hands. "But he loves you. You know he loves you! He's probably feeling so bad right now," he said, looking around to see what Morgan was up to. "I'm sure he's-" he froze mid-sentence and turned back around to face me.

"What?" I asked. He didn't answer me. "What?!" I snapped, turning around to see what he had been looking at. What I saw made my blood run cold in my veins. Morgan was sitting with Georgia on the same bench by the pond I had been sitting on with him earlier. They were laughing and drinking whiskey together.

"What the fuck," I whispered. "Is he serious right now?"

I pulled out my phone and texted him.

AUBREY 9:07 PM: What kind of sick games are you playing right now?!

I saw him pull his phone out of his pocket and check his texts. As soon as the light from the screen hit his face, I knew right away he was drunk. He squinted his eyes to read my texts and looked around, trying to locate me, in vain.

MORGAN 9:08 PM: You don't wanna be with me anyways so why do you care

I felt the anger rise in me.

MORGAN 9:09 PM: Why don't you fucking make out with him while you're at it.

I lifted my head from my phone and saw him staring at me.

AUBREY 9:10 PM: You're drunk

MORGAN 9:10 PM: Yup.

AUBREY 9:11 PM: You're an asshole

MORGAN 9:12 PM: If you say so :)

I turned off my phone and felt my eyes well up with tears.

"Hey, don't cry. They're just talking, Aubrey," Jared said softly, putting a hand on my shoulder.

"He knew this would hurt me. I'm 7 months pregnant! Why can't he just fucking act right?!" I cried. Jared pulled me into a hug and I rested my chin on his shoulder.

"Shhh, it'll be okay. I'm here," he said softly, comforting me the best he could.

"Why don't we start by getting your fucking hands off my wife, buddy," Morgan said from behind me, barely standing.

"Yeah? How about you stop making her cry so I don't have to keep picking up the pieces behind you, asshole?" Jared said, pulling away from me and getting up.

"Wanna come say that a little bit closer?" Morgan dared him.

"What are you gonna do? Fuck me up like you did Jesse back in Vermont when he found out you had been fucking his girl for months?" Jared asked defiantly. What the fuck are they even talking about?

"You have no idea what you're talking about."

"I'm the one who stitched him up you fucking piece of shit. Why do you always have to ruin everything good? Why do you fuck over every one who tries to be nice to you?! Fucking grow up man! You're 30 years old! Whiskey and girls were fun at 21! You're gonna have a fucking baby with the girl of my dreams! You knew I was in love with her! You knew I'd been in love with her for years and you still pulled that shit! And you don't see me complaining?! So fucking grow up and be the man she deserves. That's the least you can do," he said before shoving him slightly to move past him.

"Jared!" I called as he walked away.

"I'll call you in the morning, I need to cool off," he said as he kept on walking. I sighed.

"Tell me again how he's not in love with you," Morgan slurred, barely able to stand on his own two feet.

"You're drunk," I stated.

"So what?! I was still right!" He yelled, laughing to himself.

"Do not fucking raise your voice at me right now," I snapped. He sighed. "C'mon, let's get you to bed," I said, wrapping his arm around my shoulder and helping him make his way to the house. We ran into Ernest and Delaney as I was practically carrying Morgan into the house

"Woah, there. Let me do that," Ernest said, wrapping Morgan's arm around his own shoulder and carrying him inside.

"Thanks," I breathed as they walked away.

"Did you have a good night," Delaney asked, smiling at me. I sighed.

"Listen, I'm not trying to be ungrateful or anything, but the fact that you would bring Georgia to my baby shower considering what happened between Morgan and her feels kinda disrespectful," I admitted. She looked at me, mortified.

"What do you mean? What happened between them?"

"They hooked up. Before I knew him, sure, but still. You didn't know?" I asked, raising an eyebrow.

"No! God, no! I'm so sorry, Aubrey! I would have never brought her here if I had known," she said, shaking her head in disbelief. "I hope that doesn't change anything between us, I was really looking forward to having a new mom friend in Nash'. Especially one that understand my situation with Ern touring and everything, and-"

"You're fine," I interrupted her. "Obviously you didn't know. No harm done," I said calmly.

"He's throwing up!" Ernest called from the porch.

"Shit. Sorry, I have to go check on him," I told Delaney.

There, there, my darlings! Enjoy!

P.S: the amount of comments I've been getting lately truly warms my heart

XO

LadyBug

Chapter 34

I walked into the house where Morgan had thrown up all over the kitchen floor and was now bent over the kitchen sink, holding on to the counter for balance. I felt the nausea overcome me as my eyes trailed over the puddle of vomit.

"Morgan Cole Wallen, what the hell is wrong with you?!" Lesli yelled as she walked into the kitchen.

"I'm so sorry, Lesli. I'll clean everything up," I said, apologizing on his behalf.

"I better not see you scrubbing that floor, Aubrey. You're seven months pregnant and fully sober. This has nothing to do with you," she said sternly. She walked up to Morgan who was still losing balance over the sink. "Aren't you even a little bit embarrassed? To think that you're allowing your future wife to see you like this is shameful, Morgan. Go take a shower and go to bed or God help me-"

"Fine," he mumbled. "Help me?" He asked me, reaching out his hand.

"I'll get you to the bathroom," Ernest said, grabbing him. "Try to keep it in this time, man."

"Sorry," Morgan slurred. I sighed.

"I'm so sorry, Lesli," I apologized again.

"You have nothing to be sorry for, honey. If anything, I'm sorry for my son's behavior. Tonight was supposed to be your night," she said, disappointed.

"Well, I had a great time," I assured her. "And the party was beautiful."

"Thank you, darling. I'm glad you enjoyed yourself," she smiled.

"I'll go see if he's okay," I said softly. She nodded and I made my way to the bathroom where Ernest had sat him down in the bathtub.

"I'll do a lot of things for him, but bathing him is out of the question," Ernest said. I chuckled.

"I got it from here," I said. "Thanks for helping."

"Anytime," he said. He gave me a quick nod and left the bathroom. I locked the door behind him and helped Morgan get his clothes off.

"Come with me," he said, as I was running the water over his naked body. "I want you against me," he slurred. I rolled my eyes.

"I'm good right here," I said dryly.

"You're pretty," he mumbled.

"And you're drunk."

"You're by far the prettiest girl I've ever been with."

"I'm gonna need you to shut the fuck up right now," I snapped. He giggled.

"I like it when you're feisty," he mumbled. I rolled my eyes, again.

"Come in the bathtub with me, the water's nice," he begged.

"You're getting on my last nerve," I warned him. He looked down at the water and splashed me like a little kid playing in the pool. "Are you serious right now?!"

"Come with me!" He requested again.

"No!" I answered. He splashed me again. "Morgan, stop! What the fuck?!"

"You can't stay in them wet clothes, baby! You'll catch a cold," he slurred, winking at me. I looked down at my fully soaked dress and sighed.

"You're a fucking idiot," I frowned. He splashed me again. "Boy, have you lost your mind?! What the fuck is wrong with you?!" I said as he kept on splashing me.

"I'll stop if you come in with me," he giggled.

"Fine, fuck!" I groaned, taking off my dress and underwear. He stared at me.

"You're so fucking beautiful," he whispered.

"Shut your mouth. I'm freaking 30 pounds heavier than I was when you first met me and my-"

"Shhhh," he shushed me. "You're the most beautiful creature God has ever made," he said, grabbing my hand and pulling me in closer to him.

"Move," I said, stepping into the bathtub and laying down next to him. He wrapped his arm around me and we both laid on our sides, facing each other. The warm water was up to above my shoulder and I had to admit this felt nice.

"I love you so much," he said, placing a kiss on my forehead.

"Then why do you keep doing dumb shit?" I asked softly, letting the warm water slowly wash off my anger.

"I don't know. I do shit I don't mean. You hurt me and I wanted to hurt you back. I didn't do anything, Aubrey, it's not like I asked her to be here. And then when I tell you that it's like you don't believe me. It drives me nuts how you just blame me for shit I can't control. I just wanted to piss you off," he admitted.

"If I hadn't been there would you have slept with her?"

"If you hadn't been there I wouldn't even have looked at her. The only reason I even spoke to her was to piss you off, honestly."

"Is that why you got way too drunk too?" I asked, rolling my eyes. He chuckled.

"I was just hurt, I didn't wanna feel anything anymore."

I sighed. Neither of us were perfect. We both had our own baggage and share of issues, but we had to figure out a better way to communicate with one another. This wasn't sustainable. There would come a time where one of us would take it too far and we wouldn't be able to go back anymore.

"What happened with Jesse in Vermont?" I asked.

"That was a long time ago," he said.

"That's not what I asked you," I said softly, putting a wet strand of hair behind his ear.

"He's an asshole is what it is," he said, rubbing his face with his wet hands and letting out a sigh.

"How so?"

"He was dating this girl, Amanda, and he was putting hands on her. I noticed this huge bruise on her shoulder at a baseball game and asked her what happened. She started crying almost immediately and told me that

that piece of shit had been abusive to her for months. I told her I would help her," he said nonchalantly.

"And?" I asked.

"And we made a plan where I would tell Jesse that I was in love with Amanda and that she was in love with me and she was leaving him. I was just buying her time to grab her shit and leave. She was looking for a way out and I gave her one. When I told Jesse that I had been sleeping with her for weeks he hit me. So I hit him back, but he wouldn't stop. So I kind of got carried away and... knocked him out. And apparently he went to Jared to get stitched up or something 'cause now he's the good guy and I'm the piece of shit," he mumbled.

"But why are you still friends with him?" I asked, shocked by the story he had just told me.

"I'm not, but the guys are. I promised Amanda I wouldn't tell a soul and I haven't. Well, until now," he said. "But why do you think I drove out to Vermont instead of flying with Jesse and Ern? Or why I was sitting by myself at the bar instead of with them when I first met you at the baseball game? I don't wanna be around that fucking piece of trash. And when I saw your ex speak to you the way he did? Man, he's lucky there were other people there," he blurted out.

"You're a good guy," I said softly looking into his eyes. He looked back into mine, his beautiful blue eyes squinting slightly as he bit his bottom lip.

"I wanna have a million babies with you," he slurred, kissing my neck. I giggled.

"That's not gonna happen," I laughed.

"Can we practice?" he winked.

"Boy, have you seen how drunk you are? There's no way you can even get it up right now," I laughed. He frowned.

"There's other things I can do."

So, I know just by looking at my stats that some of you really like smut and some of you really don't so I'm gonna do a quick stand alone smut chapter for Ch. 35. Y'all can read it if you like it or skip it if you don't. As per usual you won't have to read it to make sense of the rest of the book.

Hope y'all like this!

XO

LadyBug

Chapter 35 (smut)

✶ *WARNING : MATURE/SEXUAL CONTENT** (As usual, if you don't like smut you don't have to read this. The story will still make perfect sense, I promise)

"I wanna have a million babies with you," he slurred, kissing my neck. I giggled.

"That's not gonna happen," I laughed.

"Can we practice?" he winked.

"Boy, have you seen how drunk you are? There's no way you can even get it up right now," I laughed. He frowned.

"There's other things I can do," he said, letting his hand trail to my inner thigh.

"Because you know you're too drunk to get hard," I teased, giggling.

"Girl, shut up before I shut you up," he chuckled.

"Oh, you think you can shut me up?" I dared.

"You think I can't?" he said, letting his fingers trail further up my inner thigh and onto my pussy. I shivered. "Already shivering?" He teased, raising an eyebrow.

"Yet, I'm still talking," I said, pursing my lips.

"How about now," he said, slamming his lips aggressively against mine. He moved his hand slightly and before I could say anything he slowly slid a finger inside me. I moaned into his mouth and felt him smile against mine. He broke the kiss, still slowly sliding his finger in and out of me. "Pretty quiet now," he teased. I sighed, letting my head fall back onto the edge of the bathtub. He slid a second finger inside me, playing with my clit with his thumb at the same time. I'm still mad at him, but fuck this feels good. I covered my mouth, trying to suppress a moan and unintentionally bucked my hips against his hand.

"Fuck, you're hot," he whispered against my neck. "I'm gonna make you cum so many times tonight."

I felt the butterflies coming alive in my stomach as he spoke those words. He went deeper inside me, his fingers reaching that sweet spot that made me squirm. He giggled at my reaction and slid his fingers out of me.

"Why are you stopping?" I asked, catching my breath.

"I want you in my bed. I want to see you. All of you," he said, pointing to the lower half of my body that was submerged under water. "C'mon," he said, grabbing my hand and helping me out of the bathtub. I got out and he covered me up with a clean towel, drying my shoulders off. I wiped the water off of the rest of my body and he slapped my butt as I walked out the bathroom. I giggled and he followed me into the bedroom with only a towel wrapped around his waist. Thankfully, everyone had gone home and both the kids and his parents were asleep. I closed the door behind us and he pushed me gently onto the bed.

"Lay down," he ordered seductively, looking a little less drunk than he had seemed when I had first walked into the bathroom an hour ago. I did as told and lied down onto the bed, the towel still covering my body. He pulled it off of me roughly.

"I told you I want to see you," he said sternly, letting his fingers run from my shoulders onto my breasts and playing softly with my nipples. I exhaled slowly and he bit his lower lip, not taking his hands off me. He put each of his hands on either side of me and let them trail down to my thighs. He opened my legs gently and looked deep into my eyes. I let my head fall back onto the bed, breaking eye contact. The anticipation was killing me. I felt his finger push against the entrance of my pussy and finally slide in. I exhaled, feeling the tension being released from my body and almost immediately felt his tongue on my clit.

"Oh f-" I stopped myself. He smiled against me, adding a second finger. His tongue slid up and down my clit and his fingers moved in and out of me repeatedly. I let out a needy moan and instantly tried to cover my mouth.

"If you keep trying to be quiet I'm gonna stop," he warned me. Damn he's hot when he takes charge like that.

"You told me to shut up," I said, reminding him of what he had said earlier. He stopped. Fuck.

"You wanna play little miss arrogant right now?" he asked, raising his eyebrows.

"I'm just saying, that's what you said."

"You want me to stop?" He warned. I shook my head no. "Then apologize right now," he ordered, looking deep into my eyes.

"I'm sorry," I mumbled.

"What was that? I didn't hear you," he said, sliding a finger back inside me. I moaned softly.

"I'm sorry," I said, a little bit louder.

"Say I'm sorry, Morgan," he commanded, sliding a second finger inside me.

"Fuck- I'm sorry, Morgan," I said, looking into his eyes. He bit his lower lip.

"Good girl," he said, winking at me. I felt a shiver go down my spine. How the fuck is he that hot. It's stupid. He put his mouth back on my clit and I moaned.

"Oh my god, don't stop. I'm gonna cum," I whispered. I felt his tongue sliding faster up and down my clit and I moved my hips against his face.

"Stop moving," he ordered, pinning my hips against the mattress.

"I'm not doing it on purpose," I whined. He put his mouth back on me and I grinded my hips against him again. He stopped.

"You want to be a spoiled little brat? Then you don't get to cum," he said, looking deep into my eyes.

"That's not fair, I-" I started, before noticing he was unwrapping the towel from around his waist. "What are you doing?"

"You really thought I couldn't get it up? You're cute," he said, taking the towel off and setting free his throbbing erection. Holy shit. "Worst part is, I would've made you cum as many times as you want," he said, rubbing his dick slowly. "But you don't wanna listen. So now, I get to have fun with you."

He spat in his hand and wrapped it around his cock, getting it wet with his own saliva. I twitched in anticipation and he pinned my hips down.

"I told you to stop moving."

"Sorry," I mumbled.

"What?" He asked, raising an eyebrow.

"I'm sorry, Morgan," I said, biting my lower lip.

"That's better," he said, slowly pushing is cock inside of me. I couldn't help but to let out a needy moan. He smiled, looking down at his dick sliding in and out of me. "You like that, don't you?"

I nodded frantically and he grabbed my hips, pulling me closer against him, allowing him to go even deeper inside me. He looked into my eyes as he thrusted his hips into me.

"I love you so fucking much," he whispered, breaking character.

"I love you too," I whispered. He pushed the hair off my face and looked into my eyes as he rocked his hips even deeper inside me, hitting my g spot with every thrust. "Shit," I moaned, closing my eyes and letting my head fall back onto the mattress. He put his thumb on my clit, rubbing it softly and taking my pleasure to a whole new level.

"Holy fuck, Morgan. Please don't stop," I moaned.

"You're gonna cum for me, baby?" he asked, biting his lip. I nodded, looking into his eyes. He pulled out his dick and put his mouth back on my clit, sliding two fingers at once inside me and tickling my g-spot with them. I felt the rush of the orgasm course through my veins. Every muscle in my body contracted and I came on his fingers, letting out the neediest moan I'd ever made. I covered my mouth, embarrassed and he pulled his fingers out of me.

"That was so fucking hot," he whispered, wiping the corners of his mouth. "Can I cum inside you baby?" he asked. I nodded and he grinned, sliding his cock back inside me and bucking aggressively into my hips.

"Fuck, you feel good," he moaned, hitting me harder with every thrust. He put both of his hands on my tits, squeezing them softly. "You're so hot, baby."

He squinted his eyes looking deep into mine. His beautiful blue eyes. The eyes that had made me fall in love with him in the first place. In that moment I felt so connected to him it was like no one else had ever been in my place. Like I was the only girl who had ever mattered to him and the only one who ever would. I felt him slow down and he grabbed my hips, pulling them harder into his.

"Fuck, I'm gonna c-"

He couldn't even finish his sentence before I felt his whole body twitch against me. The warmth of his cum filled my insides and he exhaled softly before slowly pulling out.

"You're so fucking hot," he said, laying down next to me. He placed a soft kiss on the side of my head. "I love you more than words can even begin to express."

I looked into his eyes and in that moment, I felt more in love than I'd ever felt.

"I love you too," I whispered, not breaking eye contact.

"I love you both," he said, gently putting a hand on my baby bump. "So much," he added before placing a soft kiss on my forehead. "C'mon, let's get you to bed."

So, someone compared this story to Fifty Shades of Grey so of course the nerd in me had to go and read it.... God forgive me for this LMAO

I hope y'all twisted minded folks like this! ;)

XO

LadyBug

Chapter 36

I opened my eyes and yawned, looking at the clock on the nightstand. 9:36AM. I slowly stretched my arms and immediately realized I was still fully naked from last night's... frolics. I quickly covered myself up with the blankets and Morgan chuckled softly, already staring at me.

"Goodmorning, beautiful," he whispered, wrapping his arms around me and pulling me in closer. I rested my head on his bicep, snuggling against his warm body.

"Goodmorning," I whispered softly. "How are you feeling?" I asked, gently pushing away the hair that was falling into his face.

"My head hurts a little, but having a hot naked lady in my bed does make it slightly better," he said, letting one of his hands trail down to my ass. I rolled my eyes and giggled.

"Yeah, I bet your head hurts. You really should apologize to your mom," I said, gently tracing circles on his shoulder with my fingertips.

"Why?"

"For puking all over her kitchen floor?"

"Wait, what?" He asked, shocked.

"Do you not remember?"

"I don't remember puking, I-"

"What do you remember from last night?" I asked him. He winked at me.

"I remember that," he said, pointing up and down my naked body with his index finger. He bit his bottom lip. "Do I get seconds?" He asked, grabbing my butt and pulling me in closer.

"Morgan! Be serious for a second," I reprimanded him, giggling. "Do you remember fighting with Jared?"

"Like physically?!"

"No, but you probably would have if he hadn't left."

"What did I do?" He asked. "I remember you spending the whole night with him and pissing me off. I remember sitting with that girl, Delaney's friend, and spending the whole night looking at you, wanting to rip his fucking head off, but I don't remember actually confronting him about it," he admitted.

"It's probably better that way," I stated, remembering how he had confessed being in love with me right in front of Morgan. If he doesn't remember, I don't have to tell him, right?

"Why?" He asked, raising an eyebrow.

"Because, it was a dumb fight," I lied.

"Mm," he mumbled, stretching his back. "Man, I feel like shit."

"Yeah, well, your mom is probably up with the kids. You really have to apologize," I insisted.

"Alright," he whined. He got out of bed and quickly threw on a t-shirt and a pair of jeans. "Are we heading back to Nash' today?" he asked.

"I don't know, I was kinda hoping I'd get to talk to Jared before we leave," I admitted. He nodded and left the room. I rolled over and grabbed my phone from the bedside table. 6 texts and 3 missed calls. All from Jared. I sighed.

JARED, 4:56 AM: I can't sleep, are you up? We need to talk.

JARED, 5:02 AM: You're probably asleep and I know I shouldn't be texting you but I think you're making a mistake. You shouldn't marry him. He still acts like a kid and he doesn't deserve you. The way he treats you isn't right, Aubrey. I'd never treat you like that.

JARED, 5:07 AM: If it's the baby you're worried about, you know I'd help you out right?

What the fuck is he on?

JARED, 5:09 AM: I meant everything I said tonight. He's an asshole and he ruins everything he touches. He fucks over anyone who tries to get close to him and you deserve better than that and so does Ellie.

JARED, 5:10 AM: For years I've been in love with you and I was too much of a p*ssy to make a move on you. I know the timing is horrible but it took me seeing you with someone else to realize I couldn't fake it anymore...

JARED, 5:36 AM: I'm too drunk to be sending you shit like this. Just forget I said anything...

I sighed and turned off my phone. What the fuck was he thinking? That I would just leave Morgan and ride off into the sunset with him? I couldn't believe he was putting me in this position at seven months pregnant. He knew he meant the world to me. He knew I'd do anything to keep him as a friend, but leaving Morgan? That was out of the question. Even though our relationship had its issues and we had had our ups and downs, I was madly in love with him and I knew he loved me too. I was excited to start a family with him and to get married and no amount of pressure from Jared would change that. Left my phone on the nightstand and got dressed to go check on Morgan and the kids. I walked into the living room and Ellie and Indie were playing together with their legos. Morgan was talking to his mom in the kitchen. I sat on the couch and discreetly eavesdropped on their conversation.

"I'm really sorry, 'Ma. I know I should've paced myself a little better."

"You know, she will get sick of your antics at some point. You can't be having a baby, especially a third child, and still be drinking everyday and picking fights with her every chance you get. She's patient right now, but throw another kid into the mix and a lot of things will change, Morgan. That woman has a heart of gold and you know there are other men who would kill to be in your shoes," she told him softly. Did Jared talk to her?

"Why are you saying that?" He asked. "What do you know?"

"I saw the way that boy looks at her and I know you saw it too," she stated. Shit.

"Who, Jared?" He asked. She didn't respond. "I'm not worried about him," he added.

"Well, maybe you should be. He's a good lookin' man from a good family and he seems to really care about her," she said.

"Who's side are you on, damn," he snapped.

"I'm just saying, don't give her a reason to go there. Throwing up like that in front of everybody after spending the whole night chasing another woman at her baby shower. That ain't right. I raised you better than that."

"I wasn't chasing anot- You know what, I don't have to explain myself to you. She gets it and you don't, that's fine. I'm sorry I threw up in your kitchen, thank you for the party, but we have to go," he said, obviously getting agitated. "Aubrey!" he called from the kitchen. I got up off the couch and walked towards the kitchen.

"Get yours and Ellie's stuff. Time to go home," he said.

"Morgan, I wasn't trying to upset you honey," his mom started, trying to put her hand through his hair. He took a step back swiftly.

"I'm not upset," he snapped.

"You okay?" I asked him, pretending I hadn't just heard their entire conversation.

"I'm fine," he mumbled. "Get the kids' stuff, I'll get the stuff from our room, alright?" he asked me, placing a quick kiss on my forehead. I nodded.

"Sure," I said softly. I glanced at Lesli who looked genuinely upset. "Is everything okay?" I asked her, honestly concerned. I loved his mom and the last thing I wanted was to cause conflict between them. Morgan had already left the kitchen to go pack up our room, leaving her and I by ourselves.

"Oh, it's nothing, honey. Don't you worry about me. I think I was a little too honest and I might have hurt his feelings," she said softly.

"Can I help in any way?"

"You sweet, sweet girl. There's nothing you can do," she admitted, pulling me in for a hug.

"What the fuck?!" I heard Morgan yell from our bedroom. I pulled away from the hug and excused myself to go check on him. I walked into our bedroom and he was sitting on the bed with my phone in his hands.

"Were you just gonna hide this from me?" he said, turning the screen toward me, displaying the texts Jared had sent me. Fuck.

There you go my darlings, enjoy!

XO

LadyBug

Chapter 37

"Were you just gonna hide this from me?" he said, turning the screen towards me, displaying the texts Jared had sent me. Fuck

"I wasn't hiding anything from you. I just saw this when you left the room!" I defended myself, knowing fully well I might not have told him if he hadn't found out.

"I'm gonna give him a piece of my mind," he said, throwing a sweater on and getting ready to leave.

"Woah, there. Where do you think you're going?" I asked.

"I'll let him know who he's messing with," he spat angrily.

"Can you calm down for a minute? Why the hell do you always have to be so fucking impulsive?"

"Oh, I'm in the wrong here?!"

"That's not what I'm s-"

"You know what, Aubrey? I'm getting a little sick of always being painted as the bad guy. If you think I'm such an impulsive piece of shit then maybe he's right. Maybe you'd be better off with him," he said, slightly raising his voice.

"You don't mean that."

"Oh, I mean it. Call him, tell him to come pick you up. I'm done."

"Are you serious right now?!" I asked, tears welling up in my eyes.

"Dead fucking serious."

"You told me you loved me," I whispered, my voice breaking.

"People lie. Grow up," he said. My heart sank into my stomach. How the fuck could he do this to me?! I let the tears run down my cheeks and picked up my phone. He left the room and slammed the door behind him. I sat on the floor, my legs feeling too weak to even stand on. The pain I was feeling, in that moment, was greater than I'd ever imagined a heartbreak could feel. I sobbed quietly, holding my head between my hands. How the fuck did we get here?

AUBREY, 10:38 AM: Please don't do this to me.. I love you..

I wrote as my hands trembled across the keys. I inhaled slowly, trying to calm myself down, in vain.

MORGAN, 10:39 AM: Go home, Aubrey.

I felt my heart break into a million pieces as I read that. I called Jared.

"Hello?"

"Can you come pick me up?" I sobbed into the phone, trying to regulate my breathing.

"What's going on? Where are you?"

"At Lesli's house. He doesn't want me anymore- He asked me to leave and- Ellie and I-"

"Hey, hey it's okay," he said softly, putting an end to my rambling as I hyperventilated over the phone. "Breathe in," he said, doing it with me. "There you go, breathe out," he added softly.

"I love him, Jared," I whispered, my voice breaking as I spoke these words.

"I'm on my way, alright?" he assured me.

"Okay," I whispered before hanging up.

****

I was waiting on the front porch with mine and Ellie's stuff all packed up when I saw Jared's truck pull into the driveway. He climbed out of the driver's seat and walked up to me.

"You okay?" he said softly, looking into my eyes. I nodded, giving him a faint smile as my eyes filled up with tears. "Where's Ellie?" He asked.

"Inside. I haven't told her yet that we're leaving. She's playing with her bro- with Indie," I mumbled.

"Alright, go wait in the truck, I'll get her," he said softly. I nodded.

"Thank you," I said, walking up to his truck and getting into the passenger's seat. I saw Morgan come out of the house and start talking to Jared. I couldn't hear what they were saying but I could see the conversation was getting heated. I opened the door and climbed out of the truck to hear what was going on.

"Go back in the truck, Aubrey. Everything's fine," Jared told me.

"Yeah, be a good little girl and listen to daddy, Aubrey," Morgan spat.

"Don't fucking speak to her like that you piece of shit," Jared said aggressively.

"Don't push me, motherfucker. I'll knock you the fuck out."

"Morgan," I cried. "Stop."

"Oh, stop fucking crying. I won't touch your little boyfriend," he told me.

"Jealous?" Jared taunted him.

Before I knew it, Morgan jumped on Jared and punched him in the face. I ran towards him.

"Morgan, stop," I said, trying to hold on to his shoulder to break them apart.

"Get the fuck off me," he yelled at me. Jared got back up and pushed him, which made Morgan back up and fall onto me. I hit the floor and immediately knew something was wrong. I looked down and saw a drop of blood on my jeans that quickly got bigger, and bigger. I moaned in pain and started sobbing. I stared straight ahead of me, my eyes wide opened, unable to speak or move.

"Aubrey!" Jared yelled. Morgan turned around and saw the blood coming from my crotch area.

"Shit," he whispered. "What the fuck did you do?!" He yelled at Jared. "What is wrong with you to fucking push me into a pregnant woman?!" He looked at me and I could see the fear in his eyes. "Baby, look at me," he said softly. His voice felt like nothing more than background noise. My whole world felt like it was collapsing onto itself. I could feel my whole body shaking, and yet I was incapable of doing as little as blinking.

"We have to get you to the hospital," Morgan said softly.

"Ellie," I mumbled incoherently.

"She'll be fine. I'll stay with her," Jared said.

"You're not going anywhere near my daughter," Morgan said defensively. "My mom's here, you've done enough. Get the fuck out of here," he said, helping me up.

"Morgan, I didn't-" Jared started.

"Get the fuck out of here!" Morgan yelled. Jared got into his truck and drove off without speaking another word. Morgan carried me in the truck and put me down gently on the passenger's seat, fastening my seatbelt for me. "You'll be okay, baby. I promise. You both will be okay," he whispered into my ear before placing a kiss on the side of my head. I was still staring straight ahead, unable to even make sense of what was happening. He jumped into the driver's seat and drove off, speeding his way to the hospital.

The drive could have lasted five minutes just as much as it could have lasted 3 hours. I was too out of it to even know how fast or slow time was passing. We got to the hospital and Morgan left me in the car, by myself.

"Come back," I whispered, after he had closed the door. I looked down at the puddle of blood that was covering the seat. I felt like I was frozen in time. Everything around me was slowly crumbling as I sat there, by myself, waiting to be saved or left to die. Morgan came back some time later. Maybe a minute, maybe an hour. He had some nurses with him and a gurney. He got me out of the truck and they laid me down onto the gurney.

"Ma'am, can you tell me what your name is," one of the nurses asked me. I was frozen. Unable to answer a single question, even one as simple as that.

"Her name is Aubrey," Morgan said. "She's my fiance, she's 31 weeks pregnant," he said, his voice breaking.

"I need her to answer the questions, sir. I need to see what mental state she's in," the nurse said softly as they rolled the gurney into the hospital.

"Sorry," he mumbled, barely audibly. He held my hand as they rushed me into a room and called for a doctor. Morgan got closer to my face and looked into my eyes, still holding my hand.

"I'm so sorry, Aubrey. This is all my fault," he said, his voice breaking. "I didn't mean what I said, I was just angry. You have to know that. I love you so fucking much, and Ellie, and our baby," he whispered, placing a hand on my belly gently. "Please say something. Please tell me you know I love you. I love you so much, baby," he sobbed softly. I squeezed his hand faintly, trying as hard as I could to let him know that I knew. I knew he loved me and I loved him too. I never wanted him to doubt that. Not even for a second.

"We have to take her into the operating room right now, sir," the nurse informed him. "We're gonna deliver the baby."

Y'all, I'm officially done writing this. Next chapter is the last chapter, which I will post pretty much right away. I hope you guys like this!

XO

LadyBug

Final Chapter

This story started with pain. The pain of being left alone to fend for myself and my child at 19 years old. The pain of having too much on my plate and seemingly no one to help me take some off of it. The pain of feeling worthless, unlovable, undesirable. This story started with pain and it ended with pain. The pain of seeing your 3.9 pound daughter in the NICU and not being able to hold her as much as you would like. The pain of the c-section scar, feeling like it's going to get ripped open everytime you sneeze. The pain of seeing the everlasting feeling of guilt in your boyfriend's eyes everytime he looks at you.

"She's strong, just like you," Morgan said, kissing my hand softly. "They said they expect her to make a full recovery. According to Dr. Engler, we should be able to take her home in a couple of weeks," he whispered. I smiled faintly, still under a lot of drugs, trying to make sense of everything that had happened.. "I'll go get you some water."

"Stay," I whispered, not letting go of his hand. He sat back down and looked at me. "Stay with me, please," I mumbled.

"I'm so sorry, baby. I never should have-"

"I know," I said. "You're fine. Let's forget about that. We have enough on our plates as is."

"I love you so much," he whispered, placing a gentle kiss on my forehead.

"I love you too," I mouthed weakly.

A nurse walked in and gave us a big warm smile.

"Congratulations," she said softly. "How are you doing, mom? How's the pain?"

"Bearable," I answered.

"You did a good job! Now you get to rest. If you need more pain meds, if you're hungry or you need help to go to the bathroom you just ring the bell, okay? Don't be shy, now," she insisted. I nodded. "How about you, dad. How are we feeling?" She asked Morgan.

"I'm alright, it's not like I did most of the work," he joked. She laughed.

"Would you like to hold the baby? Skin to skin contact is very important for newborns, especially preemies," she smiled.

"Could I?" He asked.

"Sure!" She answered cheerfully. "Just take off your shirt so she can feel your skin on hers," she instructed him. He looked at me as if he was trying to get my approbation. I nodded and gave him a faint smile. He took off his shirt and the nurse took the baby out of the incubator and put her into his arms. He snuggled her up against his chest and she cooed softly. I felt tears well up in my eyes.

"Hi babygirl," he said, softly stroking her forehead with his thumb. "She's so beautiful," he said, looking at me. I felt a tear roll down my cheeks.

"Sailor Lesli Wallen," he whispered. "I will love you until the day I die."

Seeing him holding our daughter like that made everything that we had gone through worth it. I realized, in that moment, that not all pain was bad pain. Sometimes, feeling your heart sink into your stomach simply meant that you cared. Love is joy, and laughter. But, it is also tears and pain. And if you do it right, if you put all your efforts into loving the right person; the person who you want to come home to at the end of the day. If you do that, then the good will outweigh the bad and the pain will feel like nothing more than a stepping stone into the life you deserve. So yes, this story started with pain, and it ended with pain. But the journey? The journey was everything but pain. And looking at Morgan holding our tiny little girl made everything that I had endured to get there worth it.

"I can't wait to marry you," I whispered.

"I can't wait either, Mrs. Wallen."